SHOOTING AT SHARPEVILLE

THE AGONY OF SOUTH AFRICA

SHOOTING AT SHARPEVILLE

THE AGONY OF SOUTH AFRICA

BY AMBROSE REEVES

BISHOP OF JOHANNESBURG

with a foreword by

CHIEF LUTHULI

illustrated with photographs

HOUGHTON MIFFLIN COMPANY BOSTON

THE RIVERSIDE PRESS CAMBRIDGE

1961

TO MY WIFE AND CHILDREN
FOR THEIR UNFAILING SUPPORT

And then was seen what we believe to be the most frightful of all spectacles, the strength of civilization without its mercy.

—MACAULAY

ACKNOWLEDGMENTS

MY GRATITUDE and thanks are due to the staff of Christian Action for typing the manuscript; to Mary Benson for much help and encouragement; to Jack Halpern for permission to draw on material already published by him; and to the editor of *Drum* for permission to reproduce a number of photographs.

Much of the work in which I have been privileged to share in these last years in South Africa would have been impossible without the continued encouragement and interest of my wife, together with the support of so many Church people in the diocese of Johannesburg, as well as numerous other friends. I have also owed much to the financial aid so readily given for defense and aid by Canon Collins and Christian Action; by the American Committee for Africa; and by the Episcopal Churchmen for South Africa.

FOREWORD

BY CHIEF LUTHULI

I WRITE WITH GRATITUDE a Foreword to a remarkable book written by a remarkable man, the Bishop of Johannesburg. He tells of times and events with which he is well acquainted, for it is to the Bishop of Johannesburg that I and many of my people have turned for advice and assistance down the years in our times of trial.

The discerning reader of this book will perceive, in the personal quality of the narrative, some measure of the part which the Bishop has played during these last tragic years in South Africa. As the chapter of events unfolds before the Bishop's pen, it becomes clear that this book could only have been written by one who knew my people and who had for them in their difficulties an infinite compassion.

The African has always been the victim of the same pattern of events: legislation with high-sounding titles, misleading to those who don't understand them, has been devised and placed on the statute book to regulate and control the African way of life. Each succeeding Act of Parliament has deprived the African of more of his rights and privileges and each Act of Parliament has been ruthlessly implemented by the government and its police force. South Africa owes much to the Bishop of Johannesburg who, through the years, has courageously and firmly drawn the attention of all who would hear to the injustice of apartheid and to the suffering that its implementation has brought upon my people.

The Bishop, down these years, received countless visits from people in distress. He gave to all such seekers for help the abiding impression that he was deeply committed to the task of bringing what assistance he could to those who required it. South Africans of every race and color found in his Lordship a true friend and a courageous ally. He is known today for his discretion, for he was the confidant of all, and trusted by all who were opposed to the government and to apartheid. The Bishop's Committee, as the group of which he was chairman came to be called, although only a liaison committee, helped to shape the destinies of many of the more positive campaigns that were fought in South Africa for the purpose of marshaling public opinion against government legislation. The Bishop, either personally or through his committee, was the architect of the multi-racial conference which made articulate and coherent the claims of the forces of liberation in South Africa. It was the Bishop who, at one and the same time, helped to bring about a solution to the bus boycott in the Alexandria township and played a considerable part in the campaign for a wage of a pound a day for African laborers. That campaign is beginning to bring relief to many poverty-stricken people throughout South Africa. Readers of this book will see how, in every time of crisis for my people, the Bishop was at hand to advise and assist them in their difficulty.

It is not surprising, therefore, that the supporters of the government have rejoiced at the deportation of this fearless opponent of apartheid. To me and many like me the deportation of the Bishop of Johannesburg has removed a personal friend. In deporting him the government has removed one of the few people who can make any distinctive contribution to the future

of our country; for he was selflessly committed to the sufferings
of the people of South Africa and did not spare himself in an
untiring effort to bring them relief.

CONTENTS

ILLUSTRATIONS

SHOOTING AT SHARPEVILLE

THE AGONY OF SOUTH AFRICA

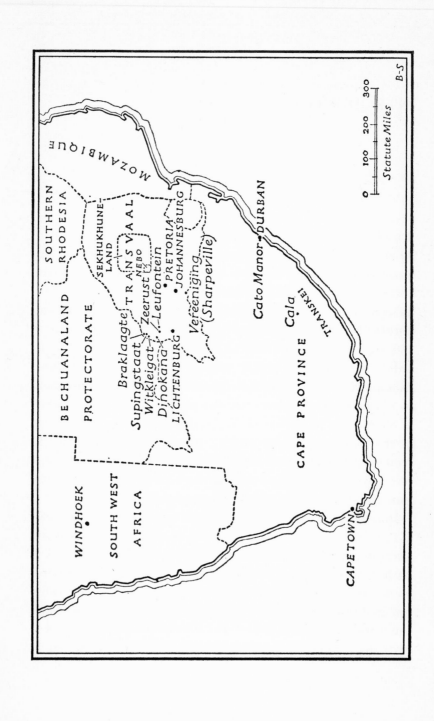

B-S

SOUTHERN RHODESIA

MOZAMBIQUE

BECHUANALAND PROTECTORATE

SEKHUKHUNE LAND

T R A N S V A A L

Braklaagte

NEBO

Zeerust

Supingstaat

Witkleigat

Leufontein

PRETORIA

JOHANNESBURG

Dinokana

LICHTENBURG

Vereeniging
(Sharpeville)

WINDHOEK

SOUTH WEST AFRICA

Cato Manor DURBAN

Cala

CAPE PROVINCE

TRANSKEI

CAPE TOWN

Statute Miles

0   100   200   300

INTRODUCTION

THE SHOOTING AT Sharpeville has shocked the civilized world. At the time of writing, the verdict of the Commission of Enquiry is not known, but it is clear that the tragedy was the outcome of the policy pursued by the South African government towards the non-white inhabitants of South Africa, who number four fifths of the population. Through the years more and more reliance has had to be placed upon the police in order to enforce this policy: whenever Africans have resisted its application the police have been employed to compel them to obey. For this reason, any discussion of the tragic events at Sharpeville must deal mainly with the attitude and actions of the police who were present, but it will be necessary to remember that the main responsibility for what happened must rest upon those who have created the mass of repressive legislation under which the non-white peoples have to live.

In order to understand the position, one has to look carefully at this policy which the police are enforcing on behalf of a white government. It is quite wrong, of course, to attribute *all* South Africa's racial and social ills to the present National Government. In many ways the present government has only taken the traditional white policies to the conclusion which, while the world may find it insane, has a warped kind of logic. For over three hundred years white policy has been directed at securing that the black man should work for the white. This has mainly been achieved in three ways: namely, the limitation of land available to Africans, the imposition of taxes, and the control, through "passes," of where the black man may seek work.

This fundamental pattern has remained unchanged to the present day, when all three factors are operating simultaneously. The pressure of overpopulation and hunger in the Native Reserves has led to unrest in the rural areas, and this pressure, coupled with the universal hatred among Africans for the "pass," which is the daily symbol and reality of white rule, has sparked off the present crisis in South Africa.

Economically, the key development in the fifty years since Union has been the transformation of a primarily agricultural and mining community into one in which already other industries contribute 30 per cent to the national income and employ a large proportion of the labor force of the country, both black and white. Too often it is forgotten that South Africa is in the throes of an industrial revolution in which it is inevitable that masses of people will move from the countryside to the towns. But most South African legislation that is concerned with race relations is a rearguard action being fought by the white authorities in an attempt to prevent the permanent urbanization of the African labor force upon which the rapid expansion, and indeed the very existence, of the new industries depends.

Three years after Union (1913) the Native Land Act already effectively confined African occupation of rural land to the Native Reserves. This had a simple effect. As close on half of the then five million Africans lived outside the Reserves, these people either had to return to the Reserves or work for the white man. In 1936 the white parliament decided to increase the area of these Reserves to 13 per cent of the land area of South Africa, but the necessary purchase of land has not yet been completed.

The first world war, which laid the basis for subsequent industrialization, threatened to upset this neat arrangement, for the additional, if limited, opportunities for employment offered by the new industries drew many Africans to the growing towns. The Land Act of 1913 did not cover this development, so, in 1945, the Urban Areas Acts were consolidated. These, together with numerous subsequent amendments, limited African occupation of land in urban areas to municipally owned and controlled townships, and later provided, under criminal penalties, for the complete control of African entry into urban areas under a provision known as "influx control." Mr. Donald B. Molten, Q.C., has rightly called these two acts "the foundation . . . of that system of color discrimination in respect of economic opportunity, participation in social services and enjoyment of civil liberties which has since become so characteristic a feature of the statute law and the administrative practice of the Union." Yet, as he also points out, neither of these two principal statutes seems to have been passed in pursuance of a general policy of segregation or apartheid, but rather on the assumption that the South African economy is dependent on black labor, that an adequate supply of that labor should be stimulated, and that the general relations of white and black should be those of master and servant.

When the Nationalists came into power in 1948, after South Africa had fought with Britain in a war in which Nazi Germany enjoyed their outspoken sympathy, they faced a new situation. General Smuts' wartime government, devoted to the maintenance of white rule, had been concerned to see that strategically important and commercially profitable new industries should be developed. They had actually encouraged the townward surge of Africans, without whose semi-skilled labor such development would have been impossible. The result was that, while there had been just over a million Africans in urban areas in 1936, ten years later this figure had grown by over seven hundred thousand. These Africans, many of whom were by then second-generation townsfolk with no tribal roots, were doing a new type of work, living a new kind of life, and beginning to make new demands.

The Nationalists saw these Africans, developing in an urban environment on which the Afrikaners exercised little influence, as enemy number one. They therefore determined to destroy the footholds of legal permanency which these people had retained. They made it their policy to bring all urban Africans under the strictest control, and, eventually, to reduce their numbers. Africans have systematically been deprived of the limited land freehold which had previously been theirs in the towns, and access to the urban areas has been brought under much tighter control. Further, two and a half million Africans live and work on white-owned farms under conditions that amount to serfdom. Most of them have no stake in the Reserves. They are not allowed in the towns. Thus they and their children must remain farm laborers.

While the government has abolished the exemptions from the pass laws which had begun to separate the African middle class from the rest of the Africans, it has also pursued a policy of divide and rule in relation to the African peoples. In 1951, without consulting the Africans, it passed the Bantu Authorities Act, which provides for the establishment of local authorities in the Reserves. This act also abolished, incidentally, the purely advisory and long ignored Natives Representative Council, which had been given to the Africans in 1936 as a sop for removing African voters in the Cape Province from the common voters roll. The important feature of the new system of Bantu Authorities is that offices of administration must be staffed entirely by officials and Africans approved by the government. The heads of these Authorities are to be the hereditary chiefs, who have been given powers to rule, if necessary, against the advice and desires of the tribe. They may exercise such powers, however, only as long as they obey the government, for the chiefs can at any time be deposed without recourse to law.

This new system has been accompanied by an emphasis on subracial purity, involving the insistence on ethnic grouping among Africans, and the attempt to unravel intertribal bonds which have come about through the years. This has been explained as a desire to "preserve and strengthen" the Africans' "own culture"; but, ironically, it has met with the most stiff resistance in just those areas where tribal tradition has been thought to be the strongest. This is not really surprising, because the Bantu Authorities system deals a deathblow at the traditional chieftainship. It makes chiefs into petty despots who exercise power as a reward for implementing government policy: where they have refused this role they have been deposed. But, here again, it is in just those areas in which tribal traditions are strongest that the Authorities have found it most difficult to find successors to the chiefs they have deposed — what that has meant in Zeerust and Sekhukhuneland will be described later.

It is this determination of the government to impose a uniform policy on all Africans, whether in rural or urban areas, that provides the link between the disturbances that have taken place in so many dissimilar districts of South Africa. This link is the South African Police, because on them rests the responsibility for ensuring that the policy of the government is carried out.

In a country burdened with an ever increasing mass of

repressive legislation, the American description of the police as a "law-enforcement agency" becomes peculiarly apt. But in South Africa such a description has to be extended. As the State has become identified with the government of the day, and the majority of the population is voteless and voiceless, "the law" becomes the equivalent of "official policy." The law must at all times be physically enforced, because not only does it lack the consent of the majority of the population, but it arouses their hostility. When this takes an overt form, the only answer the government has is to use additional force.

In a state of affairs such as this the police force increasingly takes on the functions of an army of occupation. Those who have had experience of such an army in other lands will understand more easily than others the functions the South African Police, using Saracen tanks, are called upon to perform. They will also understand the growing tendency for the police to be given wider powers of entry, search and detention many of which have been extended to the whites), and to be encouraged in the belief that they are the law.

It is now tacitly assumed by many people in South Africa that the police may enter private houses at any hour of the day or night, in most cases without being required to produce a warrant before doing so. Again and again African children see their parents turned out of their beds by the police, snatched away from them and bundled into police vans in the early hours of the morning. Most civilized people everywhere would regard such conduct as a grave infringement of the rights of citizens. It is conduct normally associated with the functions of a Gestapo.

And this sort of police activity takes on an even more serious character when it is remembered that, according to the law, no African may remain in any urban area for more than seventy-two hours unless he was born there and has resided there permanently, or has resided there continuously for fifteen years, or has worked for one employer continuously for ten years. In these two latter cases he must not have been convicted of any offense during that period. The practical effect of such requirements is that any urban African who cannot produce a permit to any policeman at any hour of the day or night on demand may be arrested. What this means in terms of the experience of Africans becomes clear when the figures in the official *Bulletin of Statistics* are examined. They show that in 1957 alone there were over a million convictions for nonserious crimes committed by Africans, and when this figure is broken down we learn that approximately 366,000 convictions were the result of infringement by Africans of laws and regulations passed for their control: over 233,000 were convictions under the liquor laws, over 28,000 convictions for offenses against the labor laws and regulations, and 393,000 for other small offenses.

The present situation can be summarized by saying that the laws prescribe where Africans may work, what work they may do, what wages they are to be paid, to what schools they may send their children, what kind of education their children may receive, in what place they may live, when they may travel and how they may travel. The major responsibility for ensuring that the African complies with all these laws rests upon the police force of twenty-eight thousand men.

Thoughtful people are even more concerned by the fact that, wide as the powers of the police are, so many of their number who commit crimes are retained in the force. Between 1946 and 1948 ninety-nine white policemen were committed for serious offenses, whereas between 1956 and 1958 the number rose to 511. In 1959 alone over three hundred white policemen were convicted of crime, but only one in five of those convicted of robbery or other charges, including assault, was discharged from the force. This state of affairs is made worse by the fact that one in three of the white police is under twenty-one years of age, and seventy-two of those at present serving are under sixteen.

It is of course true that many policemen, probably most of them, genuinely do their best to administer the law as humanely as possible; but laws which degrade the non-whites must in the end contaminate those whose duty it is to administer them. As it is hoped to show later, the final responsibility rests not upon those who administer, but upon those who frame these laws; nevertheless, discriminated against in law, regarded by most white people as less than fellow human beings, liable to instant arrest at any time of day or night on suspicion of having committed any of dozens of technical offenses which make them criminals, it is not surprising that, at the time of the Sharpeville tragedy, increasing numbers of Africans concluded that they were living in a police state.

As Brookes and Macaulay say in *Civil Liberty in South Africa*:* "The new concept of the police function tends to clothe the police force with the character of the political police of authoritarian rule. The manner in which it has been compelled to administer its function of preserving the internal security of the Union has impressed an instrument, once designed to serve the interests of justice and to elevate the rule of law, with the character of a political instrument serving the private interests of governmental power."

* Oxford University Press, London, 1959.

BACKGROUND TO SHARPEVILLE

LONG BEFORE THE tragic events of March 21, 1960, made Sharpeville a household word across the world there had been trouble with the Bafurutse tribe in the Western Transvaal.

Ever since I had first visited their villages of Supingstaat, Braklaagte and Dinokana shortly after my arrival in South Africa, these people had had a special place in my affections, for it was a joy to visit their well-ordered villages set in some of the most attractive country in the diocese of Johannesburg. I remember my first visit to Supingstaat in the days when the old Suping, then well over eighty years of age, was still alive. He invited me to his kraal and assembled the whole of the tribe over which he ruled. Although by then a very old man, he was still every inch a ruler, and I shall always remember him marching up and down in front of his people, his walking stick serving as a baton, beating time as they sang "Through the night of doubt and sorrow" to the tune of Clementine. Little did he or I know that in a few short years the Bafurutse were to experience a night of doubt and sorrow as dark as any they had ever known.

It all began when the National Government decided to appoint a new Native Commissioner. Shortly after his arrival in 1954 the Commissioner determined to implement the Bantu Authorities Act. This was the piece of legislation that, in effect,

made every tribal chief an employee of the Native Affairs
Department. Until then, Abraham Moiliva, the hereditary
senior chief of the thirty thousand Bafurutse, had refused to
accept the position. At first the new Native Commissioner
moved obliquely against him. Finding that two villages, Leufontein and Braklaagte, were situated outside the Reserve occupied by the Bafurutse, on land bought from white owners
at the turn of the century, he announced that they were "black
spots" in white areas and as such would have to be moved. As
was to be expected, Chief Abraham, with the support of almost
all his people, resisted this proposal. Taking legal advice he
led a delegation to the Native Affairs Department, from which
he received an assurance that no such move was intended. The
prestige of Chief Abraham was considerably enhanced by this
assurance, just as that of the Native Commissioner was corre-
spondingly reduced.

However, it was not long before the Native Commissioner
moved directly against the Chief. Although he was a shrewd
politician, Abraham had a fondness for the bottle, with the
result that two years earlier some of the headmen of the tribe
had complained about the laxity of his administration. Now
the Native Commissioner arranged for these charges, together
with some new ones, to be examined afresh. By October 1956
the new investigation had been completed, but no report of
the conclusions reached was ever published and no action was
then taken.

Nevertheless things did not remain quiet for very long.
Early the next year serious trouble began. On March 22, 1957,
a government notice informed the Bafurutse that the system of
reference books which had replaced the earlier passes was to
be extended to their women. For years the women had seen
the serious consequences that had followed the nonproduction

of passes by their menfolk. They knew the harassing interference with the freedom of movement of Africans that these laws could cause. Figures show, for instance, that, in the year 1957, 365,000 Africans were convicted of one offense or another against the pass laws, and as long ago as 1948 the Fagan Commission had recommended that the penalties for the nonproduction of passes should cease. The Bafurutse women knew full well that the extension of these laws to themselves would mean that they would be molested by young policemen. The chances even were that they would be detained in prison while their children remained uncared for at home.

Chief Abraham vigorously opposed the introduction of passes (or reference books) for the women of his tribe. When, on April 1, the mobile unit responsible for issuing the passes came to Dinokana, only seventy-six out of four thousand women accepted them. Three days later, April 4, at a tribal meeting that Abraham had been ordered to call, he was informed by the Regional Chief Native Commissioner that he had been deposed by the government, and was given a fortnight to leave the area. As would be expected, such an announcement stunned the Bafurutse. Certainly their "night of doubt and sorrow" has persisted from then until now.

Four months after this blow had been struck, the Native Affairs Department, after having ignored repeated letters from Abraham's lawyers, informed him that his deposition from the chieftainship had been authorized nine months before it was announced, though in fact the Department had never authorized his deportation.

For years during which the Bafurutse tribe had farmed their well-watered lands, many of the men had gone from among them to work either on farms owned by whites or in Johannesburg some hundred and fifty miles away. As soon as news reached those working in Johannesburg that their chief had been deposed and that the authorities were trying to compel their womenfolk to carry reference books, a Bafurutse Association was formed to investigate the position.

Two buses were chartered to take the investigators to their homes, and on April 13 these indignant tribesmen arrived back in the Reserve. That night most of the reference books that had been issued in Dinokana were burned, and a tribal meeting was called which swiftly became a "people's court." Four members of the tribe were branded by this meeting as informers and were allegedly condemned to be thrown to death in the seventy-five-feet-deep pit of Mamokoti. It is said that the police only intervened in the nick of time. Then the usual pattern was followed. There were mass detentions and, after a lengthy court case against twenty-three of those detained, five men were sentenced to terms of five and three years' imprisonment with hard labor for attempted murder. Women who had burned their reference books were sentenced by the Native Commissioner to fines of £150, or six months' hard labor, and men who met to discuss the deposition of their chief were arrested and fined for holding unauthorized meetings. The principal of the local primary school of twelve hundred scholars supported the issuing of reference books to women and his school was boycotted by the tribe for two days. On the third day the authorities in Pretoria issued instructions that the school was to be closed permanently, and the names of 1054 children who had absented themselves from school were circularized in order that they might be prevented from receiving any education ever again in any school. The local post office was closed down in order to protect government property, and the railway bus, which was the only link that the tribe had with the outside world, was withdrawn. Old age, widow's, and military pensions were refused to women who did not possess reference books, with the result that many of them handed in their pension books, thus permanently renouncing their meager pension of under £1 a month. Men who were unable to produce their wives' reference books found that the authorities refused to accept their payment of taxes. Young women without reference books were refused access to a marriage officer when they wanted to marry. Some women, it is alleged, were told that unless they took out reference books the district surgeon would be entitled to refuse to treat them. The Chief of Brakalulo was refused a medical examination after he had been assaulted by the police, on the grounds that the police had instructed the doctor not to examine Africans in such circumstances.

Thus retributive measures were taken by the authorities, until Detective Sergeant Jan van Rooyen appeared at the head of a mobile squad from Pretoria. Apparently this squad had been created with the specific purpose of dealing with rural Africans who resisted discriminating legislation. With his advent a reign of terror began for the Bafurutse. Operating only in the early hours of the morning, the police smashed down doors and dragged sleep-dazed African women from their beds, demanding to see their reference books, beating them, smashing their furniture and belongings, throwing them into police vans and taking them to prison. In the majority of cases they failed to obtain convictions against these women. This can be seen from the fact that, by the time a one-man Commission of Enquiry into the unrest among the Bafurutse sat on Wednesday, October 16, 1957, out of 474 who had been arrested or detained by the police, only thirty-seven had been convicted of any kind of offense.

The appointment of such a commission was also questionable. Not only was it the first time such a commission had been appointed by the national government to inquire into unrest among rural Africans, but the only public intimation that such a commission would sit in Zeerust on that Wednesday was contained in a brief announcement in the government *Gazette* on the previous Friday. Moreover, the proceedings at this commission were almost equally questionable. The lawyers for the tribe were unprepared to call witnesses and had to be content to hand in a memorandum. At the Commission a number of policemen, "loyal" chiefs, administrators, and strongly pro-government witnesses took the stand. All of them asked for the banning of the African National Congress, contending that the A.N.C. was the root cause of all the trouble that had occurred. The Native Commissioner began the clamor for this ban by handing in a list of alleged A.N.C. leaders, at the head of which was the name of the man to whom, as next in line of succession, he had unsuccessfully offered the senior chieftainship made vacant by the deposition of Abraham.

The commandant of the police in Zeerust complained of the lawyers for the defense that they had destroyed respect for the police by defending tribesmen and securing their acquittal. In a similar vein the Native Commissioner from the town of Lichtenburg in the Western Transvaal recommended that agitators should be banned without trial, since they would only make political capital out of their appearance in court. The mayor of Zeerust thought that there ought to be an army camp of five thousand strong on the Bechuanaland border: but he reserved his main attack for the Reverend Charles Hooper, Rector of Zeerust, whom I had appointed to be our Anglican missionary to the Bafurutse tribe. Some time before this attack on him the white congregation in Zeerust had tried to get me to remove Charles Hooper elsewhere. It was fortunate that I had refused, for he did much during those troublous times to retain the respect and goodwill of the Bafurutse for the Anglican Church. More than once he was accused of political activity. The truth is that during the time he was at Zeerust he exercised a pastoral ministry that will be long remembered among the African people.*

The pattern of events which emerged from this inquiry is relatively simple. Except in Dinokana, trouble only developed in the four villages in which chiefs had forced women to take reference books. The smoldering resistance of these women was fanned into flame when their menfolk arrived from Johannesburg. Then passes were burned. Once the men had returned to their work, some of the chiefs began to put into practice the lessons they had learned from the police squad which had come from Pretoria. They "smelled" out their victims, assaulted them brutally, and then handed them over to the police to be tried before the Native Commissioner. Resentment was increased by the vicious sentences that the Commissioner imposed, and by the withdrawal of social services. This resentment resulted in retaliatory arson. This in turn led to more police raids and assaults by the bodyguards of chiefs on men arriving from Johannesburg.

Perhaps the best description of the impasse that was reached is that given by Lieutenant E. H. D. Coetzee, who pointed out at the Commission of Enquiry that if all the women who did not have reference books by a certain date were ordered to be arrested, there would not be enough police to arrest them, or enough courts to try them, or enough prisons in the district to hold them. He concluded that the only way of dealing with these women was to apply a number of sanctions against them,

* A much more detailed account of these happenings can be read in Charles Hooper's *Brief Authority*, Collins, London, 1960.

including the refusal of admission of African children to schools if their mothers did not possess reference books.

The lawyer appearing at the Commission of Enquiry on behalf of the tribe was given no chance to cross-examine government witnesses, but he was invited to bring his own witnesses before the Commission on November 6. On the day before this hearing, the government issued an order forbidding more than ten Africans to gather in the Zeerust area. Unaware of this order, on the morning their own witnesses were to appear before the Commissioner more than a thousand tribesmen started along the road to Zeerust, only to be turned back at a roadblock after a brief clash with forty police armed with Sten guns, revolvers and rifles with fixed bayonets. About an hour later another thousand Bafurutse, this time mainly women, came down the same road only to be "buzzed" by eight Harvard training planes of the South African Air Force. The planes carried the day.

But the fact that the people in the Zeerust area were intimidated by such a show of force does not mean that they have been won over to the policy of the government. Many hundreds of the Bafurutse trekked across the border into Bechuanaland, and two or three hundred of them remain there until the present time, fearful to return because of their belief that chiefs favorable to the government will take action against them. Their fears are not without foundation, for in January 1958 two reporters of the *Golden City Post* were arrested on their arrival at Witkleigat by the chief there and brought before Sergeant van Rooyen. Although they possessed a press card countersigned by the Deputy Police Commissioner of the Witwatersrand the Sergeant handed them over to the chief for questioning. After they had been beaten by the chief and his men, Sergeant van Rooyen told them how lucky they were that he had been there to prevent the chief from killing them as they deserved.

Today the Bafurutse are silenced. But they have long memories. Deep in their hearts there smolder fires of resentment against those who are responsible for the night of sorrow that descended upon them. All this was the result of government attempts to compel the womenfolk to carry passes, and to move a number of families from land they had occupied for more than half a century, while deposing some of their chiefs.

II

The Bafurutse were not the only rural Africans to experience this kind of treatment by the police, at the command of the authorities. Away in the Lulu mountains in the Eastern Transvaal there lies the loosely defined area of Sekhukhuneland. Here live the Bapedi people, almost the last of the African tribes to be conquered by the white man in South Africa. Their last great chief, Sekhukhune I, had successfully amalgamated the Bapedi with the surrounding Baktoni and Batau peoples, permanently binding them into a unity. So successful indeed was his work that, while each tribal group kept its own name, the Baktoni people fought alongside the Bapedi tribe against the Burgers' Transvaal Republic from 1876 to 1878, although disputes over the succession were not settled until 1883. From that time the intertribal Bapedi, Baktoni and Batau peoples lived in peace until the passing of the Bantu Education Act in 1954.

By this act practically all African education which had been in the hands of the non-Roman churches passed into the hands of the government. Among the many schools then taken over was the mission school run in conjunction with the Jane Furse

Hospital which, until then, had been under the care of the Community of the Resurrection, an Anglican community of men who had come to South Africa from Mirfield. One of the first acts of the Native Affairs Department after taking over this school was to abolish the three high school classes in it. This, coupled with the arrogant manner in which the local authorities enforced stock restrictions and imposed new local taxes, led to considerable resentment in Sekhukhuneland. It was therefore not surprising that, when a few months later Dr. Verwoerd, then Minister of Native Affairs, held a meeting in the Eastern Transvaal to explain to the chiefs and councilors the blessings of the Bantu Authorities and the Bantu Education Acts, the people of Sekhukhuneland were not impressed. Their Regent returned home and gave his impressions to the tribe. They rejected the whole system of Bantu Authorities, and a four-year struggle with the government began. A network of spies and informers was established throughout the territory, but with little success. In June 1956, the tribe met again to consider the Bantu Authorities system, and once more decisively rejected it. So serious had the situation become that in November of that year Mr. C. W. Prinsloo, Chief Information Officer of the Native Affairs Department, came to promise the Bapedi a railway bus service, a new secondary school, a clinic, a post office and a telephone if they would accept the Bantu Authorities Act. But the tribe refused. Rumors spread that the Regent was going to be deposed, so the tribal council dismissed its secretary and head councilor whom it suspected of intriguing with Prinsloo. He was replaced by a senior member of the royal house; but after one month in office he was deported by the authorities. Still Mr. Prinsloo continued his efforts, and it appears that he finally succeeded, for in July 1957 the setting up of a Bapedi-Bantu Authority was gazetted. This led to eight thousand members of the tribe gathering at Mohaletse, where they presented to the Native Affairs Department officials a petition, bearing thirty thousand signatures, requesting the return of their exiled "sons."

No attention was paid to this petition. Certainly two new secondary schools were established, but the tension continued to increase, and in November matters came to a head. On November 29, 1957, the Bapedi Authority was disbanded for lack of support and the next day the regional Chief Native Commissioner informed the Regent that he was deposed for a month. At the same time seven men were arrested, and two of them — one of whom was the new tribal secretary — were at once deported. It is interesting to note that one of five others who were imprisoned on a charge of obstructing the authorities subsequently made application to the Supreme Court on December 4. There his lawyer alleged that the police had refused to give him access to his client. The matter was settled out of court, after ready access to the accused had been promised, and the State agreed to bear the costs of the application. In February 1958 three of these five men were acquitted and small fines were imposed on the other two men.

But before this happened the government decided to reverse the growing together of the Bapedi and the Baktoni that had been in process since the beginning of this century. The Baktoni were removed to the Nebo part of Sekhukhuneland and placed under their own native commissioner.

At the end of 1958 the suspension of the Regent was extended for a further three months, and the government, which was by then experiencing the resistance of the Bafurutse in the Western Transvaal, began to increase its pressure upon Sekhukhuneland. Acting under a law passed in 1927, Dr. Verwoerd took powers on February 28, 1958, to seal off any Native area.

Within such an area any person who "verbally or in writing makes any statement which is either intended or likely to intend to subvert or interfere with the authority of any State official or which consists of or contains any threat that any person will be subject to any boycott, or violence, loss, disadvantage or interference because of his obedience to affairs of the State" becomes liable to a fine of £300 and three years' imprisonment.

On March 7, 1958, this proclamation was applied to that part of Sekhukhuneland in which the Bapedi live, as well as to the Bafurutse people. It is understandable that such a proclamation has made it extremely difficult since that date to obtain reliable information of events in Sekhukhuneland. But the public measures taken by the government since then speak for themselves. On March 11 the Regent won a Supreme Court appeal against his suspension, on the grounds that the government had not given him the chance which the law provided of defending himself. But the very next day after he had won his appeal the government again suspended him, this time under another law which contained no such provision. Five days later the African National Congress was banned as an illegal organization in Sekhukhuneland. Anyone who even gave the form of greeting that is used by the African National Congress at once became liable for a fine of £300 and three years' imprisonment. On the last day of March the Regent was deported without any warning, together with his wife and one child, to Cala in the Transkei, many hundreds of miles from his home. Shortly after, on April 11, 1958, the Bantu Trust, which is in effect the Native Affairs Department, took over all the functions of the defunct Bapedi Authority.

One would have thought that such actions would have crushed all resistance by the Bapedi, but this was not so, for at Easter the primary school at Mohaletse was permanently closed because it had been boycotted, and it is alleged that the three hundred children who were pupils were debarred from every other school. Heavy police reinforcements were moved into the area. An attempt was made to appoint a retired police sergeant as acting Regent, but the tribe refused to accept him. The boycott of schools increased, with the result that more and more police were drafted into the area, headed by a special mobile column under Detective Sergeant J. H. van Rooyen, who was already notorious for his activities against the Bafurutse.

All this increased the tension until, on May 16, 1958, the inevitable shedding of blood began. On that day an armed police detachment arrested a minor chief who had been threatened with deposition because of his opposition to Bantu Authorities, together with his brother and a senior councilor. What happened subsequently was very terrible, but it followed a sadly familiar pattern. Apparently the villagers rushed up and held the police van into which the men had been placed so that it could not be driven away. The police claimed that the crowd began to throw stones at them, and that they were reluctantly forced to open fire in order to defend themselves. Four men were shot dead, and six men and one woman were injured. The police van sped away, and the enraged crowd began to take vengeance on those who had collaborated with the government. For several days assaults and arson followed. Seven more tribesmen died and many were seriously wounded.

Convoys of fresh police were rushed to Sekhukhuneland under the command of high-ranking police officers. Many arrests followed, and on May 26 another proclamation appeared in the government *Gazette* which made the carrying of dangerous weapons, including heavy clubs and knives, an offense punishable by a year's imprisonment and/or £100 fine or whipping. From then until now it has been almost impossible to secure much reliable information of the course of events in Sekhukhuneland, for even reporters who enter the territory do so under the strictest official supervision.

But perhaps the appearance of Mr. C. W. Prinsloo in a territory occupied by Sten-gun-carrying police provides a fitting epilogue to this sorry tale. He explained the real cause of the trouble in Sekhukhuneland: he declared that the twenty thousand Bapedi were trying to maintain an "Assegai empire" over 280,000 Baktoni, and were therefore against the progress brought by the new chiefs who had been appointed by the government. But he assured the Baktoni that they need not worry as the government would protect them from oppression. And this was in a place in which for seventy-five years the Bapedi and Baktoni had lived peacefully as neighbors!

III

Yet, serious as events have been in parts of the Transvaal, mounting tension and outbursts of unrest have by no means been confined to this province of the Union. They have not even been confined to the Union of South Africa. Disturbances have also occurred in Southwest Africa. By Article 119 of the Treaty of Versailles Germany renounced all her rights over German Southwest Africa, and these rights were transferred by a mandate to "His Britannic Majesty, to be exercised on his behalf by the Government of the Union of South Africa, to administer the Territory." It is true that the Union of South Africa has always maintained that this mandate expired with the disappearance of the League of Nations. At the same time the International Court of Justice has made three recommendations during the last eight years confirming that, though South Africa is not legally bound to place Southwest Africa under trusteeship, she is accountable to the United Nations for her administration of the territory.

Year after year lengthy discussions have taken place at the United Nations on the subject of Southwest Africa, but these have achieved very little. Meanwhile the South African Government has pursued its own course there, for all practical purposes treating the territory as if it were a fifth province of the Union. Not that the African people in Southwest Africa have accepted such a state of affairs without protest. On April 19, 1959, they formed the Ovamboland People's Organization which is open to all Southwest Africans irrespective of race or color. Its aim is to remove all racial discrimination in Southwest Africa, to place the country under the trusteeship of the United Nations Organization and to secure its ultimate independence. In September of the same year the South-West African National Union was formed with similar objectives, together with the aim of combining all the people of Southwest Africa into one political unit.

As a result of an appeal for legal help received from Chief Hosea Kutako after the shooting of eleven Africans and the wounding of many others in Windhoek Location on December 10, 1959, a lawyer was sent from Johannesburg to present the case of the Herero people to Mr. Justice C. G. Hall, who had been appointed to act as a judicial commissioner to inquire into the incident. On arrival at Windhoek this lawyer applied to the manager of the Non-European Affairs of the Windhoek town council for permission to enter the Old Location to consult with members of the Herero tribe who wished to give evidence. Apart from being taken to the scene of the disturbance by officials, he was refused permission to enter the Location for any purpose. In particular, the manager specified that he could not take statements from witnesses in the Location. This added greatly to his difficulties, as indeed did the fact that, on his arrival, he was followed by members of the Security Branch of South African Police who took the names and addresses of those of his clients who met him at the airport.

Handicapped though he was, he soon discovered that the cause of the disturbance that led to the shooting on December 10 was the resistance of the inhabitants to their proposed removal from the Old Location to Katutura. The Native Commissioner maintained that the only reason for removing them was to take them out of their hovels. The people there readily admitted that their conditions of life were deplorable, but pointed out that these were due to their cruel poverty. The policy of implementing apartheid in Southwest Africa meant that restrictions were imposed upon them which made it impossible for them to obtain better employment at higher wages.

On November 30, 1958, a meeting had been held at the office of one of the officials at the Location, attended by the then superintendent and members of the Advisory Board and of a committee that had been formed to assist the Advisory Board. At this meeting, it is alleged, it was said that the removal of the Location would take place in order to facilitate the implementation of apartheid.

The leaders of the African people maintained that it would have been possible to build new houses for them in the Old Location, if their economic position had been improved sufficiently to enable them to pay any increased rental resulting from the rebuilding. In fact, two model houses had already been built in the Location to show the residents the type of accommodation that was proposed. The Africans believe that this project was not pursued because European houses were built right to the borders of the Old Location: they think, in other words, that the real reason for moving them is the objection of the authorities to whites and non-whites living in close proximity to one another. Nor are they impressed by the argument that, as there will be industrial expansion near Katutura, it is better for Africans to live near the factories. Apart from the fact that they are not all factory workers, they naturally resent being regarded as inanimate assets for future industrial expansion, to be moved without their consent wherever and whenever they are needed.

Most of all they take exception to apartheid being introduced into Southwest Africa with neither the consent nor consultation of the African people. They believe that the South African administration is designed in the interests of the white people, and they point out that it is always the Africans who have to be moved to suit the convenience of the white people, for this is not the first time that they have been moved. At one time the Hereros lived where the "Native Hospital" in Windhoek now stands. The Namas once lived where the government buildings are now. Similarly, the Hereros once occupied Angeikas and Fort Enwalte. They were forced to move to Orumbo in 1921 and to the Amanuis Reserve in 1925. To them Katutura means "we have no permanent home."

The Africans also underline their present condition of great poverty. In the Old Location rentals were 3/6 a month. In Katutura they will be raised to £2 a month. Further, they could walk to their work from the Old Location, but Katutura is a sixpenny bus ride from town. In their Memorandum, submitted to the Commission of Enquiry, they proceed to list other reasons why they resent being moved, namely, that they will not be granted freehold tenancy in Katutura; that they are not represented on the Windhoek town council; that ethnic grouping will be strictly applied there; that the regulations which will be enforced in Katutura will be unusually restrictive on the inhabitants. In support of this last contention they point out that officials may at any time enter their homes; that the Superintendent must be given forty-eight hours' notice of any proposed "assembly of persons"; that no person may collect money from another without the Superintendent's permission; that there is no security of tenure for the inhabitants; that entrance to Katutura will be strictly controlled; that nonpayment of rent will not merely be a basis for a civil claim but will constitute an offense.

It was to be expected that resistance to the proposed Location would increase as time passed. And that it what happened. The *Windhoek Advertiser* of November 2, 1959, stated: "The natives are almost unanimous in their refusal in moving to Katutura, judging from the spontaneous response towards the Action Committee deputation." Day by day the opposition of the residents became more obvious until, on December 3, 1959, a large number of women marched on the Administration Offices following the arrest of four of their number. Eventually, as a protest against the move, a boycott was organized by the two political organizations which had been formed during the previous year. By this boycott the people pledged themselves not to use buses, beer halls, the cinema or dances. Timed to begin on December 8, it was entirely successful.

Then, on December 10, a meeting was called by Mr. de Wit in the Sybil Barker Hall in the Old Location. With him were the Mayor and other officials, Major Lombard of the South African Police, members of the Advisory Board, and interested Africans. In his speech Mr. de Wit pointed out that all municipal services in the Location were paid for out of the profits on the beer hall, and warned the Advisory Board that they would be held responsible if they allowed the people to disobey the law. The Mayor then addressed the meeting, telling them that if the people did not want municipal services he would close the beer hall and withdraw the buses. He further intimated that this would be done the next day if the boycott continued, and the services would not be restored. After further speeches, Major Lombard also addressed the meeting. He pointed out that the towns belonged to the white people and that any Africans who did not wish to obey the law in the towns must return to the Reserves. They must not demonstrate against the police as, if they did, they would be knocking their heads against a brick wall. A member of the Advisory Board tried to explain who was responsible for the boycott, but he was not allowed to do so.

Later on the same day a large force of police entered the Location. A crowd of Africans gathered in front of the Police Station, apparently curious to know why the police had arrived. It was quite an orderly meeting. The Vice-president of the South-West African National Union approached Major Lombard and asked why the police had come. He was told that they were there to maintain law and order. Then Major Lombard ordered an African policeman to tell the crowd to disperse within five minutes as they were causing an obstruction. The Vice-president pointed out to Major Lombard that such a large crowd would not hear a spoken order, and proceeded with other officials of the South-West African National Union to persuade the crowd to disperse. While this was being done the police opened fire and the crowd began to run away. Some Africans started to retaliate by stoning the police, but eleven Africans were killed and fifty others were wounded, some of them seriously. Thus was "law and order" restored to Windhoek.

IV

No account of the unrest and disturbances in southern Africa
that culminated in the shooting at Sharpeville would be complete without some description of the riots at Cato Manor
outside Durban; especially as, since the events at Sharpeville,
more than one spokesman for the South African Government
has linked the two affairs.

For a long time life in Cato Manor had been marked by an
uneasiness which found expression on Wednesday, June 17,
1959, when a demonstration was staged at the beer hall, where
a group of African women destroyed beer and drinking utensils.
The police dispersed the women and the beer hall was closed.
Some days later, the director of the Bantu Administration Department met a crowd of two thousand African women at the
same place. The spokesman for the women told him some of
their grievances, and he then addressed them. Once the meeting had concluded, the police warned the women to disperse,
and then, when they failed to do so, proceeded to make a baton
charge. This was followed by general disorder and rioting, during which a number of shots were fired. As the afternoon wore
on, the women were joined by the men, many of whom had returned from their work in Durban. Around 5.30 P.M. they
began to destroy municipal vehicles and buildings, causing
damage that was later estimated at £100,000. There is little
doubt that teenagers and a hooligan element were to some extent responsible for the looting and destruction of buildings
that took place. Five hours after the destruction had begun, a
police picket was attacked by Africans and driven off by Sten
guns. Although no official casualty list was issued, the press
reported that three Africans were killed and fourteen injured,

as well as one policeman who had been wounded by a bullet.

As no public inquiry has been held into the causes of the riots at Cato Manor it is not at all easy to determine them with any certainty. At the same time, the director of the Bantu Administration Department in Durban was confident that the basic issue was poverty. He said, "I wish to make bold and say that whatever reasons have been advanced are of a purely superficial nature. Even the women who started off this tragic course did not express their grievances in terms of bare, basic and intrinsic facts. They have talked about Kaffir beer and illicit liquor, transport and housing, shack removals and influx control, the keeping of livestock and the keeping of husbands, gambling dens and shebeens. They have talked about these subjects as if they mattered for their own sakes. Only here and there did the real, naked reason break to the surface—money or rather lack of it . . . The basic and ultimate reason is an economic one. The poverty of the urban Bantu; the discrepancy between his earning capacity and his cost of living; his inability to meet the demands of modern times in a city modeled on the Western way of life; his inability even to meet the barest necessity of life, to feed, clothe, educate and house himself and his family." Few would question the accuracy of his diagnosis in drawing attention to the grinding poverty under which the majority of urban Africans live. Yet the other causes to which he referred, while secondary, cannot be dismissed as of little or no importance.

After these disturbances the city council of Durban, together with other bodies such as the South African Institute of Race Relations, did a great deal to ameliorate conditions. But it is now a matter of history that unfortunately such steps as were taken did not prevent the recurrence of the disturbances. One Sunday afternoon in February 1960, the smoldering resentment of the Africans in Cato Manor again burst into flames, with the result that nine policemen lost their lives. This was a deplorable occurrence for, by any standards, it is impossible to attempt to justify the behavior of the crowd in Cato Manor in taking the law into its own hands as it did. Even though it appears that the persistent raiding for illicit liquor, passes and permits during that week had subjected the inhabitants to great provocation, it has to be recognized that these policemen lost their lives in the execution of their duty, and the immediate blame for their deaths rests upon those who murdered them.

Less immediately, much of the blame for Cato Manor must also belong to those architects of apartheid who have striven in so many ways during these last ten years to enclose the whole life of the African people within the strait-jacket of compulsory segregation.

As I write, the same pattern of events has manifested itself in Pondoland, where about thirty people have been killed by police action and many more wounded. The government has prevented lawyers instructed by the Pondos from appearing on their behalf. Bantustans and Bantu authorities have been rejected by the Pondo people as indeed by the Xasa people of the Transkei. My information is that the Commissioner appointed to the territory has warned the government that this rejection may take the form of widespread resistance which he will not be able to combat.

SHOOTING AT SHARPEVILLE

SINCE MONDAY, March 21, 1960, the name of Sharpeville has become almost a household word around the world. As far as African townships go, Sharpeville can truly be described as one of the best-planned and most reasonably conducted Locations in the Transvaal. It is a Location of which any municipality might justly be proud, at least as far as the general layout and standards of housing are concerned. The Anglican Church there and in the surrounding districts is so strong that we now have three African priests working in the area. But all that had been built up laboriously through the years was severely strained in a few moments on that fatal Monday morning. Looking back on it, one is bound to ask why the tragedy should have happened at Sharpeville, of all places.

It is easy to give a simple answer — namely, that the trouble flared up over passes. Unquestionably, as with the unrest among the Bafurutse, passes were the immediate cause, though technically there is no such thing as passes, because they were replaced by reference books under the Abolition of Passes Act, 1952. In the reference book are consolidated all the details which were previously entered on various pass documents. It contains the holder's name, his tax receipt, his permit to be in an urban area and to seek work there, permits from the Labour Bureau, the signature of his employer each month, and other particulars, such as the fact that he is exempted from carrying a certain type of pass. In spite of the Fagan Commission recommendations, the reference book must be shown on demand to any policeman or any of the fifteen different classes of officials who require to see it. Failure to produce it on demand constitutes an offense. If an African cannot produce his book he may be detained for not more than thirty days while inquiries are being made about him. In many towns there are regulations which make it necessary, in addition, for an African to carry a special pass from his employer if he is out at night after a fixed time. If he hasn't a special pass he can be arrested by a policeman without any warrant being issued.

Nobody who knows these facts needs much imagination to realize why such laws arouse violent feelings of resentment, and the worst has not been told. The position is gravely aggravated by the manner in which the laws are administered in the Native Commissioners' Courts. To say this is not to make any accusation against those who preside over the courts, for they are placed in an impossible situation, which becomes clear when it is realized that a thousand Africans are charged every day of the year with offenses under the pass laws. If found guilty, these offenders either have to pay fines ranging from £5 to £8 or go to prison for a period ranging from five to eight weeks. On the morning I spent at one of the courts, cases were disposed of with great rapidity; few were discharged and fewer still received a nominal fine of £1. It has to be remembered, too, that even those discharged lose valuable time from their work, and by their absence risk the loss of their employment. Recently there has been some improvement in the working of the courts, largely because of representations made to the authorities and the presence of a rota of white people in some of the courts to observe what is happening: in fairness to those administering the laws, it is only right to say that they are more than anxious to improve their administration wherever possible. None the less, the situation remains barely manageable.

But I had known from information received from within Sharpeville that tension had been increasing there for some time for other reasons, mostly connected with the fact that wages in that area are low and rents are high. Prior to March 1960 certain rents had been increased. In addition, many people whom I spoke to complained that the "dom pass" was being used as an instrument for the restriction of the free movement of labor. A person dissatisfied with the terms of his employment could not leave his employer to seek better conditions of labor without running the great risk of being endorsed out of the area by the Pass authorities, thus losing not only the opportunity to work at all, but also his right to a house and home for his family. Although a scientific study has not been made of this subject in the Sharpeville area, it is useful to examine the findings of a study of urban Africans in Johannesburg made on behalf of the South African Institute of Race Relations* — the probability is that the situation of urban Africans in Sharpeville is worse than that obtaining in Johannesburg. This study shows that the poverty datum line for a family of five Africans in Johannesburg is approximately £24 per month, but to maintain such a family adequately requires at least £36. In actual fact, some 80 per cent of the African families a year ago had a family income of under £20 a month, 8 per cent between £20 and £25 a month, and only 12 per cent had an income of more than £25 a month. If it is asked how families live on incomes which in many cases are so far below even the minimum requirements, the answer is simply that somehow they manage to exist only at the expense of depriving themselves of the food necessary to maintain them in health.

African wages remain low, partly because African Trade

* *The Cost of Living for Urban Africans*, Joy de Gruchy, 1959.

Unions are not recognized for the purpose of bargaining with the employers, and also because, for various social and economic reasons, their productivity is low. Further, in the present political setup in South Africa, the color bar in industry secures high minimum wages for the skilled white workers and low minimum wages for the unskilled black workers. All this means that in South Africa there are two wage structures—black and white—and in the fixing of the former the workers frequently have little or no say at all.

Several weeks before the tragic events at Sharpeville it was obvious that the economic situation in which the inhabitants found themselves, as in many other urban areas, was rapidly becoming intolerable. It is far too easy to explain what subsequently happened as the result of agitators and intimidators. It is high time that those in authority in South Africa realized that agitators find it extremely difficult, if not impossible, to stir up a contented people. All that they did in Sharpeville was to exploit a situation which, for economic and political reasons, was already highly explosive, and a large measure of responsibility for this state of affairs must rest on the governing group in South Africa.

Their responsibility also extends to the activities of the agitators themselves, for the simple reason that, by banning and banishment, the authorities have for some years been silencing and crippling the effective leadership of the African National Congress, which is committed to a policy of nonviolence. At the same time, until just prior to Sharpeville, when they rounded up most of the leaders, the authorities had allowed the pan-Africanists, a powerful splinter group of the African National Congress, to continue their activities unchecked. Some of us had been mystified by this policy, and had concluded rightly or wrongly that, as in their attempt to foster tribalism,

this policy was actuated by their belief that the most satisfactory
way to maintain white supremacy is to divide the Africans
among themselves. Knowing something at first hand of the
rival policies of the African National Congress and the Pan-
African Congress, I realized that the pursuit of such a policy
was fraught with immense dangers. Unfortunately, as we shall
see, events at Sharpeville only too clearly demonstrated the
truth of this conclusion.

II

On the morning of the shooting a crowd of Africans assembled
round the Police Station in Sharpeville and, whatever the true
story of what happened may be, the fact that has never been
questioned is that the police opened fire. Sixty-seven Africans
were killed and 186 were injured.

During the months before Sharpeville, Robert Sobukwe, the
leader of the Pan-African Congress, and his lieutenants had
proceeded throughout South Africa calling upon Africans to
arouse themselves to resist the pass laws. As far as could be as-
certained later, some days before the disturbances in Sharpeville the party took over whatever political organization had
formerly existed there in readiness for the launching of the
campaign, and called for action. The leaders announced that
they themselves intended to hand in their passes to the Police
Station on March 21, and during the weekend immediately
preceding that fateful Monday they distributed thousands of
leaflets throughout the township calling on people to stay away
from work on that day and to hand in their passes. The same
leaflet called on Africans to abstain from violence.

Early on the morning of March 21, members of the Pan-
African Congress proceeded through the streets of Sharpeville

knocking on doors and waking up the occupants of all the houses. Many Africans joined in the procession willingly, but others felt compelled to leave their houses and go along with the Pan-African Congress. At the same time, members of the Pan-African Congress had prevented the bus drivers from going on duty, and so, on the morning of March 21, there were no buses to take the people of Sharpeville to their places of work. During the night and in the early morning, meetings of Africans had been held throughout the township. While the police say that hundreds of stones were thrown at them by a very large crowd of Africans in the streets, and that on one occasion they were fired upon by Africans, there is other evidence which shows that peaceful meetings of Africans were violently broken up by the police. It was difficult to find people who had been injured by the alleged stoning, as only two policemen said that they were injured during the night.

Many people started out to work on bicycles and on foot, but met parties of organizers, some of whom threatened to burn their passes or to "lay hands on them" if they did not turn back. There appeared to be no concerted plan of action by the Pan-African Congress. Few people were sure whether they were supposed to gather, and where, and groups of Africans drifted throughout the morning to various points in the township, such as the superintendent's office, the hostels and the school square, as well as to the Police Station. Gradually the news spread through the township that a statement concerning passes was to be made by some important person during the day at the Police Station, and from about eight in the morning Africans started to gather around it. A large group had gathered in Seeiso Street near the school, and this group was eventually persuaded to move up the street and to join those who had gone to the Police Station. There, Africans waited patiently for the expected announcement and gradually the crowd grew.

Various estimates have been made of the crowd, and it would seem that, although there must have been a gathering of some thousands of Africans, press reports and the South African Police almost certainly overestimated the number. The Prime Minister read the official Police report on Sharpeville to the House of Assembly on the evening of March 21, 1960. In this report, the allegation was made that there were 20,000 people round the Police Station. The photographs which are included in this account show pictures of the crowd at various times throughout the morning, and it seems unlikely that there were more than 5000 people in it at any one time [Plate 8].

As the crowd gathered, it seemed to concentrate mainly on the southern and western sides of the Police Station between the small gate in the southern fence (this gate opened into Zwane Street, which is the street with the island shown in the photographs) and the large gate in the western fence which opens into the street running between the Police Station and the Clinic. Some people gathered along the fence on the northern side of the Police Station, and there were other groups at the southern corner and along the eastern fence. These people went to the Police Station for a variety of reasons. Many were present because they wished to participate in a protest against the pass laws: others were there because they had been intimidated, out of idle curiosity, or because they had heard a report that an address was to be given about passes. As far as I can ascertain, no policeman ever asked the crowd why they had come to the Police Station, nor did any policeman ever ask the crowd to disperse, even though their presence at the Police Station seems to have caused an unnecessary amount of alarm.

At about 10 A.M. aircraft flew backward and forward, diving down over the crowd, presumably in order to get them to disperse. If this was the intention it did not succeed because the children cheered the planes, and many more people, seeing the aircraft from a distance, were attracted to the Police Station to see what was happening. I am not aware of the cost to the government of putting a squadron of aircraft into the air, particularly when among those aircraft there were jet fighters. It does seem to me, however, that the aircraft represented a very expensive method of dispersing a crowd which would probably have gone home if a policeman had taken the trouble to ask them to do so. No police officer has contended that the crowd was ever ordered to disperse except when Captain Brummer made an attempt to address a portion of the crowd in English.

Eventually, Tsolo — the Secretary of the Pan-African Congress organization in Sharpeville — was seen to go and talk to Lieutenant Visser of the police, and the word spread that he had been told that a "big boss" from Pretoria would speak to the crowd at about two o'clock. On hearing this, some people left the crowd for a time, to go to the cafés for refreshment or to return home to listen to the radio; many of them returned to the Police Station at about 1.30 P.M.

What sort of crowd was this which gathered at the Police Station? The Prime Minister told the House of Assembly that it was in a riotous and aggressive mood, that it brandished weapons and stoned the police. I do not believe that this is true. Many eyewitnesses to whom I spoke told me that the people gathered about the Police Station were in a happy mood. Very few Africans had gone to work, and an idle, holiday atmosphere pervaded the town. Some were singing and occasionally some shouted slogans. I have been told that the crowd were not carrying weapons, and that no one was carrying stones. After all, they had not gone to fight with the police but to protest against the passbooks. The photographs I have included show the crowd during the morning, and particularly just before the shooting. These pictures clearly demonstrate that it was unarmed, and that it was composed, to a large extent, of women and children. Quite apart from the evidence of African witnesses, there is the evidence of European photographers who were present at the Police Station: they testified to the fact that they had no difficulty in moving among the crowd and taking their photographs. The illustrations also show that, up to a short time before the shooting, those police who were in the Police Station appeared to be unconcerned; they made no defensive preparations to hold the crowd back, and apparently from eight o'clock until the time the shooting broke out no attack was made upon them. It seems that there were members of the crowd who waved sticks, but here again, the photographs show an almost complete absence of sticks.

Mr. Labuschagne, the Location Superintendent, who is *the* man of authority in Sharpeville, says that he walked through the crowd at about 1 P.M. and climbed over the fence. He says that he met with no hostility, but, on the contrary, was greeted in a friendly manner and chatted with some of the people. There were policemen who were prepared to say that the crowd was in fact so great and so hostile that it was only with the greatest difficulty that they drove their Saracens through it — among them were Captain Brummer and Captain Van der Linde. Unfortunately, their drivers, Sergeant Van der Bergh and Constable Arnold, who were looking through the same periscopes, said that they found no difficulty in driving their Saracens into the Police Station; indeed, the photographs show that almost the entire width of the street was unoccupied, and that this "angry" crowd was engaged in various peaceful occupations. Some people were even sitting down.

As time wore on, the crowd increased. Nobody seems to have

been waiting very purposefully, and although the crowd was making a cheerful amount of noise, shouting to one another and singing, no one that I spoke to saw any signs of violence or preparation for an attack on the Police Station.

During the morning, the police at the station were gradually reinforced. At 10.30 A.M., the total number did not exceed six white and six non-white policemen. Thereafter, some African constables arrived, and later, nearer 11 A.M., Lieutenant Visser came to the Police Station with a few more men. It was about 11.30 A.M. that Captain Van der Linde took two Saracens to the Police Station. One Saracen was placed inside the fence near the southwestern corner, while the other returned to the Municipal offices which are situated near the gates of the township. At about 11.45 A.M. Captain Theron brought in a further twenty-five white and African policemen. The numbers grew even further with the arrival of Captain Brummer and three more Saracens. He was accompanied by Lieutenant Colonel Spengler and Colonel Prinsloo of the Special Branch of the police, who brought yet more armed and uniformed policemen. Still later, nearer a quarter past one, Lieutenant Colonel Pienaar arrived, together with Lieutenant Claassen and a further contingent of armed men. It is of interest that, apart from a conversation which Lieutenant Visser had with Tsolo, the police seem to have had no further contact with the crowd, and were apparently content to stand or stroll about the grounds of the Police Station, or in the inner yard, or in the Police Station itself.

As I have said, no one asked the crowd to disperse, and the police took no action to arrange for the defense of the Police Station. Surrounded as they were by this crowd, the police strolled about with their rifles slung over their shoulders, smoking and chatting to one another. The photographs bear out these facts. I also believe that at no time were the gates locked or barred, and for long periods of time no policeman was even stationed as a guard on the West gate. When Captain Theron arrived, he did not even go round the perimeter of the station, or into the Police Station itself to see what forces were available to him, while the senior officer in charge, Major Van Zyl, left the Police Station at 11.30 A.M. and did not return at all. Photographs show police cars which brought the senior officers entering the gates. The gates are wide open and a few policemen are to be seen standing next to the motorcars, chatting and smoking or smiling. While all this was going on, Tsolo and More (another Pan-African leader) had spent their time urging the crowd to stand away from the fence in order that they should not damage it, and had continued to do so throughout the morning until Tsolo went to get some lunch [see Plate 9].

Lieutenant Colonel Pienaar arrived at the Police Station under a number of very serious misconceptions. He had been told by Major Van Zyl that he was coming to face a most dangerous situation. He believed that earlier in the morning attempts had been made to disperse the crowd at Sharpeville station by means of a baton charge and tear gas and that the crowd at the Police Station had fired shots at the police. This information was quite incorrect and Major Van Zyl said so. Worse still, however, after his arrival, Lieutenant Colonel Pienaar did not discuss the situation with Captain Theron or any of the other officers who were present. He had one very cryptic conversation with Captain Theron in which he asked what Captain Theron thought of the situation. Captain Theron replied, "Colonel, you can see for yourself."

As far as I can see, Colonel Pienaar made no effort to investigate the situation that existed, nor did he consider using methods of persuasion on the crowd which would not only have been effective, but would also have been humane and civilized. He did not ask why the crowd was there or what they were waiting for, yet it seems highly probable that, if he had known the crowd was waiting to be addressed, the tragedy of Sharpeville might have been avoided. Lieutenant Colonel Pienaar himself admits that he did not know, nor did he inquire whether hoses or tear gas were available at the Police Station. Although Lieutenant Colonel Pienaar had nearly three hundred men in his command, he did not think that a baton charge would be of any use. In fact it is difficult to ascertain what Lieutenant Colonel Pienaar did understand or know about the situation, for he did not know how many men he had under his command or what armaments they possessed. He seems to have spent thirty minutes arranging his policemen in a line, and even this is disputed. I quote from the evidence of the Commission when it was put to Lieutenant Colonel Pienaar that he could have tried to disperse the crowd by an order. He said: "I did not have any time to do that. I would have liked to."

Counsel, instructed by me, then put it to Lieutenant Colonel Pienaar: "You would very much have liked to, but in the whole of that half hour — and we know what you did during that half hour — in the whole of that half hour you could not have spared a minute and a half in order to make this humane effort?"

Lieutenant Colonel Pienaar: "No, I could not."

Counsel then asked, "And you have no explanation for that, except the explanation you have already given us?" — to which Lieutenant Colonel Pienaar replied, "It would not have taken minutes to make other arrangements."

Counsel then put it to Lieutenant Colonel Pienaar: "I am suggesting, Colonel, that you could have climbed onto a Saracen in your striking uniform and held up your hand for silence — and perhaps they would have been silent. And then you could have said, 'Now, go home or you are going to be shot.' You could have done that, couldn't you?"

Colonel Pienaar's reply was: "The only explanation I can give is that time did not permit that."

Counsel was not prepared to let Colonel Pienaar evade this issue and said to him: "You could have done that, couldn't you?" Lieutenant Colonel Pienaar replied, "I could, yes."

Counsel: "And your only excuse is that you were too busy doing the other things that you have told us about?"

Lieutenant Colonel Pienaar: "Yes."

Counsel: "Colonel Pienaar, you could have detailed some other officer to make that effort, couldn't you?"

Lieutenant Colonel Pienaar: "I could have, I did not think of that."

About a quarter of an hour after his arrival, Lieutenant Colonel Pienaar gave the order that the men should fall in. There was some confusion about this, but ultimately the police were in a long line about five yards form the fence facing the crowd on the western and southern sides, while on the northern side there were three Saracens. A little later Lieutenant Colonel Pienaar said, "Load five rounds." He said nothing more to any of the officers, nor to the men. He made no attempt, either, to divide the men into sections, nor did he place any officers or N.C.O.s in control of any particular group. The police did not even fall in in the groups in which they had arrived at the Police Station, and the Sten-gunners chose their own position in the line. Many of the men had already loaded their weapons with the full number of rounds they could hold. Colonel Pienaar says now that he knew that many of the men had loaded, but he thought that his order would frighten the crowd. He says that the order was an indication to his men that, if they had to fire, they should not fire more than five rounds. No one can be surprised that, if this was the intention of his cryptic order, it was unfortunately not understood by the policemen in his command.

Colonel Spengler during this time busied himself with the arrest of two of the leaders of the Pan-African Congress. These were the persons who had been present in the Police Station grounds most of the morning; namely, Tsolo and More. Afterwards Colonel Spengler went to the West gate and arrested another man. Spengler says, and he has told the Commissioner so, that it was perfectly reasonable for him to carry out these arrests. While the crowd was a little more noisy than it had been earlier, he did not think that it was intending to storm the Police Station. When the African constable opened the gate for him to carry into effect his arrest, part of the crowd was pushed against the gate by the weight of the people behind. There was, however, no difficulty in pushing the crowd back and closing the gate again. When subsequently he arrested a man in a red shirt he again did not feel that the crowd was in a violent mood, nor did he believe that the crowd was angered by the removal or arrest of these people. A few moments later, another man offered himself for arrest, and Colonel Spengler asked the African constable at the gate to open it.

What happened next is exceedingly difficult to know for sure. Some of the members of the crowd who had been near the gate said that they heard a shot, some that they heard a policeman say "Fire." Others just suddenly became aware of the first unexpected volley. The police were firing into their midst. All said that they turned and ran with everyone else just as soon as they realized what was happening, for the general surprise seems to have been so great that a few remained for a second or two in stunned amazement, unable to comprehend that the police were really not just firing blanks. They were quickly disillusioned. Yet Lieutenant Colonel Pienaar is quite clear that he did not give the order to fire, and he says, moreover, that he would not have fired in the circumstances, himself.

The result of the firing was devastating, and the figures which were established later, both at the post-mortem inquiries and by the hospital, show that over 70 per cent of the victims were clearly shot from the back. At the very most, only 15 per cent of the wounds were inflicted from the front. Many of the crowd who saw the police start to raise their weapons began running immediately, and most of the bodies of the dead and dying fell in the road immediately in front of the western fence and in the field to the north and northeast of the Police Station. The body of the woman shown in the illustrations (see Plate 22) was lying well over one hundred yards from the fence. One woman in the hospital told me that she was in a shop buying groceries when she was shot, while another woman said that she had been hit while doing her washing in her back yard.

Those people who were wounded at the shops and on the northern side were victims of firing which broke out from certain policemen standing on the top of the Saracen tanks. These policemen are shown in the photographs. The man in the center originally denied that he had ever fired his Sten gun, but in the original ammunition return made after the firing he is reported to have stated that he had fired thirty-five rounds; the photographs show him not only firing his Sten gun, but also reloading it and firing again (see Plate 15). The firing seems to have gone on for some forty seconds or more. During that time, 705 rounds were fired, seven men firing ten rounds each with their rifles, and one man firing twelve rounds. At least four men fired twelve rounds each from their revolvers, and one man fired nine. In each case, the man concerned must have fired all six rounds from his magazine, broken open his revolver, taken the cartridges from his pocket or pouch, and reloaded. Several of the Sten-gunners appeared according to the returns to have fired two complete magazines, one having reloaded and fired seven rounds from a third magazine. Two policemen, not satisfied with firing two complete magazines from their Sten guns, then changed from Sten guns to their revolvers and fired six rounds from them.

Some of the external and internal injuries caused by these bullets were so extensive that an inquiry into the cause of them was desirable. Because of the unsatisfactory nature of the returns, the police were unable to say clearly what ammunition was used, but it would seem that these wounds were caused either by ricochets, or by the fragmentation of bullets, or by the fact that Sten gun bullets struck the bodies of the dead and wounded in a tumbling position. Whatever weapons were used, the massacre was horrible. Some of the victims were youngsters and there were women and elderly men among the dead and wounded. Many had been hit in the head or stomach and were terribly mutilated. One such man, John Mailane, father of a large family, had his head blown off while distributing invoices for his firm on his bicycle, some distance away. Another man, passing by in the street to the north, suffered such severe injury to his leg that it was later amputated. These were not dangerous agitators, but for the most part ordinary citizens who had come to see what was going on [see Plates 16–23].

To make matters worse, some of the wounded say that they were taunted by the police as they lay helpless in the street, and were told to get up and be off. Others who tried to help were driven away and told to mind their own business. Initially, the only person who was present to help those who lay dying and wounded in the midday sun was the Reverend R. Maja. He had been drinking tea in a nearby house when the firing broke out, and he gave what help he could. I have attached his evi-

EVIDENCE FROM THE
PHOTOGRAPHS

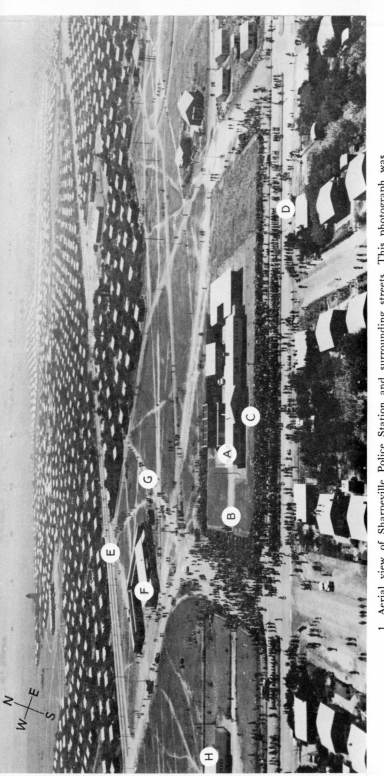

1. Aerial view of Sharpeville Police Station and surrounding streets. This photograph was taken on the morning of the shooting: note the thin crowd and people walking away.

A. Police Station
B. Main entrance
C. Side entrance
D. Zwane Street
E. Seeiso Street
F. Cafés and shops
G. North field
H. Clinic

2. Saracen passing unmolested through the crowd about one and a half hours before the shooting.

3. Saracens approaching the Police Station along Zwane Street about three quarters of an hour before the shooting. They are accompanying police vehicles which took Colonel Pienaar and Lieutenant Colonel Spengler to the scene.

4. Cheerful men, women and children outside the south entrance about half an hour before the shooting. Note that the solitary African constable (wearing a topi) has his back to the crowd.

5. Outside the Police Station about half an hour before the shooting; the crowd is thin. These people are giving the "Afrika" sign, raised arms and thumbs up.

6. This is what the police described as an armed mob. One man has a stick and there are a few umbrellas.

7. Captain Brummer spoke of driving through a "wild" and almost impassable crowd, attempting to enter the Police Station. This photograph of the scene on the west side was taken immediately after his arrival.

8. The South African Prime Minister alleged that the Police Station was surrounded by about 20,000 people. Another view of the crowd on the west side.

9. Police car entering main gate. Note (a) sjambok (the police denied carrying sjamboks); (b) crowd leaning on the fence.

10. The police stand talking with their backs to the fence, yet they claimed that this was a dangerous crowd.

11. Shooting has begun on the west side. Plates 11-15, taken from the northeast, are part of a series of twelve made during the firing. The filming time and distance covered by the runners are evidence of its duration.

12. Note police with their backs to the crowd and the number of children: they would hardly have been brought if a fight had been expected.

13. Yet now it is necessary to fire with revolvers and Sten gun.

14. None of those fleeing carries a weapon.

15. Note that a police constable is reloading.

16. and 17. Two views from inside the fence, facing southwest, immediately
after the shooting. Note that the police have not yet come out,
i.e. no weapons have been removed.

18. Part of the west fence which the police alleged had been pushed over.

19. Two policemen have now come out. Note that the heads of the dead point away from the Police Station, in the direction they were running.

20. The southwest corner of the fence where the concentration of people was greatest.

21. Victims of the firing from the Saracens in the field north of the Clinic, 50–100 yards from the fence.

22. This body is about 150 yards from the northwest corner of the fence. Note that the woman was shot from the back and the entrance wound was small.

23. The same woman seen from the front. Note the extensive bleeding from the exit wound: the types of wounds inflicted in the shooting were remarkable.

24. Items collected from the scene by the police — shoes, hats and other articles of clothing. Note buckling of the south fence. This is Zwane Street where no police were drawn up.

25. The Rev. Maja giving water to a man who later died.

26. The scene in the street some time after the shooting.

27. Ambulance from Vereeniging. Note the policeman with a sjambok.

28. Outside the Police Station a considerable time after the shooting.

29. Police survey the scene.

30. Africans look on in misery and disgust.

dence, together with that of some of the other witnesses, by way of an appendix to this book. Later, cars and ambulances arrived. The dead were loaded into trucks and the wounded taken to hospital.

III

All through that day I tried, in vain, to establish contact by phone with the African Rector of Sharpeville, Father Voyi. It was only on the following day that I learned that telephone communications had failed because the cable to Sharpeville had been cut.

It was almost impossible to obtain any reliable news of what had happened, and it was only on the following morning, Tuesday, March 22, that I became involved in this tragic event. On that morning I was attending a meeting in Johannesburg when a friend, who had just arrived from Pretoria to stay with us for a few days, brought a note from my wife asking me to telephone the Anglican Chaplain at Baragwanath Hospital. This I did and learned from him that the situation there demanded my immediate attention. Because of what I was told, I decided to take a senior lawyer with me to Baragwanath.

Arriving at the hospital we were met at the gate by the Anglican Chaplain — a member of the Community of the Resurrection. To him, as well as to other brethren in this Community, the Church owes a tremendous debt for the unfailing care and compassion bestowed on those wounded at Sharpeville during the days and weeks they were in Baragwanath Hospital. They were untiring in their ministry. Perhaps it was an omen of subsequent events that the vehicle to follow us into the grounds of the hospital was a large police pickup van.

After a few words with the Chaplain, we went together to

discuss the situation with several of the senior medical staff. From them I gathered that there were a hundred men, thirty women and six children in various wards of the hospital as a result of the shooting on the previous day. These were the bare facts of the situation; but my general impression was that the members of the medical staff whom I interviewed were disturbed by what they had seen: they appeared more shaken than I would have expected them to be as experienced medical men.

After this conversation I went with our Chaplain to visit the injured. The scene was extraordinary. Outside each ward there were a number of African police, some white police and members of the Special Branch in civilian clothes. In the wards I talked with some of the wounded while the advocate I had brought with me spoke with others who could only speak Afrikaans. I learned from members of the Community that the injured were deeply concerned about their legal position and that they desired legal representation in order that they might be advised about their position. I then promised those who asked for this assistance that the full cost of legal advice for them would be met from the fund that was being established for the purpose, and that I would arrange for attorneys to visit them to take their instructions.

It was clear that many of the people there were afraid of what would happen to them when they left the hospital. For this reason we decided to try to make an appointment with the Deputy Commissioner of Police. But this proved impossible, so the advocate and I decided that after lunch we would go to his office and ask to see him. We sat in the outer office for a short time as we were told he was on the phone. On the conclusion of his telephone conversation, we were told that the Deputy Commissioner could not see us, as he was then going to town. At this the advocate explained that we wished to discuss

certain aspects of the Sharpeville case with the Deputy Commissioner. The officer returned to the Deputy Commissioner
to explain our business. After a moment, he told us that the
Deputy Commissioner would give us two minutes. The interview was so unsatisfactory that, on its termination, I instructed
a firm of attorneys to send the Deputy Commissioner a letter
setting out the details of our interview.* On my return to
Johannesburg I immediately arranged for the same attorneys to
represent me in regard to the shooting, and asked them to
proceed to Baragwanath Hospital to take instructions from the
injured and to minute their statements. This they began to do
on Wednesday morning until they were prevented by the police
from continuing their work. About two hours later they were
allowed to proceed.

On the Tuesday evening I had received a phone call inform-
ing me that the bodies of the Sharpeville victims had been
brought to the government mortuary in Johannesburg. By this
time my attorneys had been approached by dependents of some
of the dead in Sharpeville for advice and assistance, and I was
informed that it was very necessary that permission should be
obtained for a qualified pathologist to attend the post-mortem.
I was advised that this might not only throw further light on
the type of wounds inflicted and the type of ammunition used
by the police, but could also establish entry and exit wounds
caused by the bullets. On the instructions of the dependents,
and with my concurrence, an approach was therefore immediately made to the Senior District Surgeon of Johannesburg,
Dr. Friedman, for permission for our medical representative to
attend the post-mortem examinations. Dr. Friedman said that
he had no objection to a medical representative being present,
provided the police consented to this arrangement. Accord-

* See page 86.

ingly, on Wednesday morning my attorneys telephoned the police and spoke to Colonel Olivier, who refused to agree to our suggestion and said that an application would have to be made by the dependents to the Magistrate in Johannesburg. I knew that the post-mortem was due to start on Thursday morning and so it became urgently necessary to find and bring the dependents of the dead from Sharpeville to Johannesburg in order that they could be taken before the Magistrate. With the help of the Reverend Maja, some of these dependents were found, and tribute must be paid to a number of white women who, at very short notice, drove to Sharpeville through all the police cordons, past the Saracens, to fetch the grief-stricken and deeply shocked relatives to Johannesburg.

The first application was made at four o'clock that afternoon in the name of Mrs. Lydia Mailane, whose husband's death I have already described. The bringing of these applications was greatly facilitated by the co-operation of the Chief Magistrate of Johannesburg, Mr. Silk, and his staff, who were prepared to wait long after court hours in order to hear the applications. By five o'clock, eight orders had been granted in favor of the relatives, giving permission for Dr. Shapiro to attend the post-mortems on their behalf.

The next morning, the same white women went again to Sharpeville and brought back more of the relatives, and a further twelve orders were obtained. As I shall show, the presence of Dr. Shapiro at the post-mortems greatly assisted my submissions to the Commission, and it became possible for the Senior District Surgeon to deal with each one in such a way that the information we sought became immediately available to us. In the end, the medical evidence regarding the nature and extent of the wounding was common cause between the Crown and the representatives of the dependents. It was this initial investigation which went so far to prove that more than 70 per cent of the persons at Sharpeville had been shot from the back.

I was visited on Wednesday by a reporter from the *Rand Daily Mail*. To him I put the request that a judicial inquiry should be established to examine the events at Sharpeville, and I suggested a number of questions which I believed ought to be discussed: these were questions that had arisen from conversations I had previously had both with members of the staff at Baragwanath and with a number of the injured. Among other things, I asked that, owing to the nature of some of the wounds, the particular type of bullet used should be investigated. I never attempted, either then or subsequently, to give any answer to this question. Whenever I was asked by members of the press if I had any particular type of bullet in mind, I pointed out that I had not. I had no intention of making any allegation against anyone: my only purpose in putting this and other questions was to demonstrate the urgent necessity of investigating most fully the happenings at Sharpeville, and this was just one of the points that I thought ought to be cleared up if and when a judicial inquiry was held.

On Thursday morning, reading in the press that the attorneys would only be allowed to interview wounded persons if they were accompanied by a policeman, I decided to visit Baragwanath again. I discovered that a number of the injured, as they were able to sit up, had been removed to the Y.M.C.A., which had been turned into a ward; so I went there first with the Chaplain. There turned out to be no truth in the report in the press, and the attorneys, now three in number, were busy taking statements from those who had asked for legal aid. I returned then to Wards 1, 3 and 9 of the hospital and talked with a number of the wounded.

Everyone to whom I spoke seemed stunned and mystified by

what had taken place. This crowd had not gone to the square expecting anything serious to happen. All agreed that they knew of no provocation — nothing to have sparked off the savage police fire—whereas, on their own side, it was claimed that the political organizers had continually insisted that there should be no violence or fighting.

Now, three days later, the sense of stupefaction and grief still remained, and Chief Luthuli sent to tell me to let it be known that he was preparing a day of mourning the next Monday, March 28, when he would be calling on his people to stay away from work once more.*

IV

On my way from the wards I was informed by the Medical Superintendent that he had had instructions that no unauthorized person could enter the hospital and that, therefore, I could no longer visit there. As we were talking, we were joined by the Secretary of the hospital. I informed him that I should have no alternative but to tell the press that I was not allowed to visit patients who were members of my own church. He asked me not to do this, but rather to consult with high-ranking officers of the Police Force. So I returned to the office of the Medical Superintendent in order to phone the Deputy Commissioner of Police. He was not available, so I then telephoned two colonels in turn who assured me that what I had been told was correct. However, I was advised to make a call to the Colonel-in-Charge of Newlands Police Station who had issued the instructions. He was most courteous and said he saw no reason why I should not visit Anglicans who were among the wounded, but that he would have to consider the matter. Not long after-

* See page 142.

wards he phoned to say that I could visit Baragwanath at any time.

As a result of the impressions I had gained at Baragwanath Hospital I decided to call together the representatives of the Consultative Committee of the fourteen organizations of which I was chairman. This meeting took place on Thursday evening and began with the reading of an eyewitness account of the Sharpeville disturbances, which was subsequently published in the London *Observer* on Sunday, March 27. By this time the attorneys had taken statements from one hundred of the injured Africans in Baragwanath Hospital and two of the attorneys present reported on the information that they had received. They also gave the results of twelve post-mortems which had already taken place; but the Consultative Committee did not discuss these results, as it was felt that no good purpose would be served by doing so while the post-mortems were still being carried out.

In the main, the statements taken by the attorneys merely corroborated what I had already been told. A few of those questioned had said that policemen, either black or white, had told them to go to the Police Station, and this statement puzzled the Committee greatly, as it was difficult to understand why such allegations had been made against members of the Police Force. It was also clear from the statements that there was no idea of violence in the minds of the members of the crowd. To support this, they confirmed that for a week before the event their leaders had told them that they must not be violent, even if they were provoked. Moreover, they pointed out that they would not have allowed women and children to be present if they had expected fighting. The first incident mentioned in these statements was the arrest of the African outside the Police Station gate. In this scuffle the man fell, and it was alleged that he was kicked when on the ground. Yet it appears that even this did not unduly disturb the crowd, and even when the police were drawn up in line and raised their weapons many said that they were not particularly alarmed. At that moment, however, the attorney reported, an African policeman apparently pushed his way to the front and shouted "Run—they are going to shoot." There was a burst of firing as he was still speaking; people began to fall to the ground. It was then that all turned and ran.

Following this report there was some discussion, and the Committee instructed me to take whatever steps I could to make these facts known to the public both in South Africa and overseas. I explained that it might be difficult to secure publication of the statements here, both because the eyewitness account referred to earlier had not been published in the local press, and because I had the impression that the reports that *had* appeared locally had largely relied upon statements made by the police. I also pointed out that, even if my impression were false, local editors were in the great dilemma that they might be accused of incitement if they published the accounts as given to us that evening. I pointed out, however, that several pressmen from overseas had asked me to meet them later that evening and that, if the Committee wished, I could give the information to them, in the hope that if the overseas press carried their impressions these would later be reproduced in the South African papers. To this the Committee agreed, as they were anxious that the widest possible publicity should be given to the account of events at Sharpeville as seen through the eyes of the injured. The Committee believed that this was particularly important, as many of the witnesses were still so ill that they could not possibly have communicated with the injured persons in other wards, yet there was remarkable agreement

among their statements. And this agreement was only less remarkable than the divergence of their statements at almost
every point from the accounts that were being given in the
press from other sources.

Late that evening a small group of pressmen met me at their
own request. To my surprise, the following morning I was attacked in one of the morning papers because I had not invited
local reporters to this "Press Conference." As no press conference had been held I was at a loss to understand the reasons for
the attack. Fortunately the South African Press Association
allowed me an interview with one of their senior representatives, and decided to use in its entirety, in cables both overseas
and to all South African newspapers, a statement I made on
the subject.

The Press Association report then went on to quote my out-
line of the significant points arising out of the affidavits obtained by the attorneys at Baragwanath Hospital, and, finally, to
enumerate the conclusions at which we had arrived:

> Speaking on behalf of [his] Consultative Committee of four-
> teen organisations, [Bishop Reeves said] they had arrived at
> the following four conclusions.
>
> (1) It was necessary that proper methods of controlling
> crowds should be introduced by the Police, which would not
> endanger life.
>
> (2) The time had come in South Africa when a clear distinc-
> tion must be made between the Army and the Police Force.
>
> (3) They believed that the crux of most of the difficulties
> was that there was no effective consultation between the author-
> ities and the non-European leaders. For instance, on the night
> before Chief Luthuli issued his call to the Natives to stay at
> home next Monday, Luthuli asked the Bishop to convey this
> information to the Progressive and Liberal Parties. He did
> this because these were the only two political parties in South

Africa which had had continuing consultations with the non-white leaders.

(4) They believed that the Government had shown by its actions this week that it had no knowledge of the true state of affairs in the country. Citing an example of this, the Bishop said that the Government's declaration that the disturbances this week were an attempt at an organised revolt was a clear illustration.

"We are deeply disturbed at the complete lack of contrition on the part of the Government and their successive attempts to justify the action taken by the Police," said Bishop Reeves. "At the same time, we are very anxious that people overseas should realise clearly that there is a sense of shock among a growing number of white South Africans with what has happened. We are anxious to convey to people overseas knowledge of the fact that all white people in South Africa are not tarred with the same brush. "

So closed an unhappy episode in what until then had been ten years of cordial relations with the press in Johannesburg. But it did not by any means close the Sharpeville incident as far as the Consultative Committee was concerned. Steps were taken immediately to set up a Defense and Aid Fund, and many white citizens of Johannesburg supplied quantities of food and clothing which were sent to Sharpeville and distributed to those in need.

v

If the authorities had admitted that a ghastly mistake had been made at Sharpeville and indicated that they intended taking steps to prevent a recurrence, the probability is that, once I had called for a judicial inquiry, I should have hesitated to make any further comment. But in point of fact the authorities adopted an entirely contrary attitude. Since the events at

Sharpeville, they have been at pains both to justify the action that was taken and to commend the conduct of the police. More recently, they have gone so far as to make it plain that, if similar circumstances should occur in the future, the police will not hesitate to shoot again.

In spite of my interview with the Deputy Commissioner of Police in Sharpeville on the day after the shooting, the police, not satisfied with the injuries which they had inflicted, proceeded to arrest all those wounded who were not critically ill. These people were taken to the cells with their wounds still stitched and undressed. After numerous postponements over a period of four months, seventy-nine people, most of whom had been among the injured, were charged with public violence. At the commencement of the trial which is still proceeding against twenty-three of them, the Public Prosecutor was obliged to withdraw against the remainder as the Crown could prove no case against them.

Perhaps there is some significance in the fact that, in statements which have been made by members of the government, the incident at Cato Manor in which nine policemen lost their lives has more than once been linked with the events at Sharpeville. While it is true that there were certain parallels in the background to Cato Manor and Sharpeville—as, for example, the economic position of the inhabitants — the incidents were dissimilar in so many respects that it is dishonest to suggest that they were identical. As I have already made clear, neither the continuous police raids nor the harrying of the inhabitants by the authorities can ever be held to have justified the Cato Manor crowd in causing the death of nine policemen in the execution of their duty. It might be much more honest and just to compare the happenings at Sharpeville not with those at Cato Manor, but with what happened at Windhoek on December

10, 1959. Although at Windhoek it was the threatened removal of the Location to another site which precipitated the demonstration, the circumstances were in some respects strikingly similar. In both cases those present declared that the demonstration was a nonviolent expression of disapproval. In both cases the police were present in large numbers. In Windhoek it is claimed that the crowd did not hear the order to disperse. At Sharpeville many of those injured denied that any order was ever given to disperse: if it was given, they did not hear it. In Windhoek many alleged that they went to the Police Station because they were curious to see why such a large body of police had come into the Location. Some of the injured at Sharpeville declared that they had gone because they wanted to see the Saracens. As one injured woman told me, with a wry smile, "I had never seen a Saracen. But I was shot before I saw one."

Why, finally, do we attach such special importance to the shooting at Sharpeville?

In the atmosphere of charge and countercharge which followed Sharpeville, many people have forgotten what is the abiding tragedy, the loss to hundreds of children of parents and the hope of education and financial support for the future. Many of the injured suffered severe injuries which will not only cause them much suffering during the remainder of their lives, but will also shorten their expectancy of life. Others lost limbs. It should be realized that an African who is maimed in this way finds it extremely difficult to obtain sheltered employment for the future. The loss of a leg to an African laborer often means no employment and slow starvation for his remaining days. Such is the fate of the children of Constance and Ethel Maisilo. Two fine women, whose husbands were brothers who ran a taxi service in Sharpeville. Twenty children have lost their fathers and these two households have lost a combined income of £80 a month. John Khota lost his right arm, shattered by machine-gun fire. John was a painter by trade and at the age of seventy was a vigorous and well-preserved man earning £35 a month. His injury has lost him his livelihood. Today, he is at a loss to know how he will fend for the future. John Marobi has lost a leg. He was a passer-by in a nearby street. Another young African lad who worked in a bookseller's is sterile, while Benedict Griffiths, whose father serves with the South African Police, only has the use of his limbs by the grace of the medical staff at Baragwanath Hospital who were indefatigable in their attempts to save him. Joshua Motha, a bus driver with a large family and earning £8 a week, lies in Baragwanath Hospital with a broken femur which will not heal. So 216 families and over 500 children are paying the dreadful price of forty seconds of uncontrolled firing at Sharpeville. The toll of irresponsibility finds its expression in amputations, severe abdominal wounds, arthritic conditions, the loss of mobility and cohesion in limbs, wives left widows, and children fatherless.

From the statements of the attorneys, conversations with many of the injured, as well as the reports of the evidence given at the Judicial Enquiry, it is difficult to avoid the conclusion that the shooting that day in March was both deliberate and unnecessary, and a great debt is owed to those lawyers in the Enquiry who presented to the presiding judge another version of the events than that given in evidence by some of the police. As Mr. Kentridge said, "We will ask you to take special note of the most deplorable feature of the proceedings in front of you—that of the deliberate fabrication or suppression of evidence by some of the police in an attempt to conceal the truth about the shooting at Sharpeville."

The demonstrations at Windhoek and Sharpeville were both dispersed by the use of firearms with a consequent killing of some of the crowd and the wounding of many others. Such a show of force, it is claimed, was necessary for the restoration of law and order. Certainly order has been restored, but it is dubious if, at a time when the normal processes of law were suspended under the South African Emergency Regulations, anyone could claim that the rule of law had been restored. And it is even questionable how far the mounting use of force, the arrest of most of the responsible African, Indian and Colored political leaders, and the dislocation of commerce and industry by the calling up of a number of regiments can be termed the restoration of order. The probability is that such a use of force will ensure that no further demonstrations will take place in the near future. But it would be a great mistake to equate such a calm with a restoration of order in South African society. Beneath the outward calm, there is a growing resentment — not only of the government, but of the dominant white group as a whole — and a firm resolve on the part of many Africans to carry on the struggle as and when it becomes possible for them to do so.

Many people will be inclined to dismiss the events at Sharpeville as just another incident in the long and growing series of disturbances that have marked the attempt to put the theory of apartheid into practice. Their only desire will be to get back to normal as soon as possible. Superficially, this may easily be achieved; but underneath the external calm, dangerous fires will continue to smolder, fires that can never be extinguished by a show of force, however invincible that force may appear to be. History, I believe, will recognize that Sharpeville marked a watershed in South African affairs. Life can never be quite the same again for any racial group in the Union, because of what happened on that Monday at Sharpeville. Outwardly things may go on very much as before. At the same time the fact that this may be so ought not to mislead anybody. A few days before Sharpeville, a Pan-Africanist said, "The tree of freedom is watered with blood." When I heard these words, I certainly did not expect they would so soon take on such tragic meaning. Yet they mean that the choice becomes ever more clear. Either there is a complete abandonment of the present policy in South Africa, or the coming years will bring increasing strife and sorrow.

THE COMMISSION OF ENQUIRY

SHORTLY AFTER THE shooting in Sharpeville the South African Government, through its High Commissioner in London, Mr. Van Rhyn, said:

> According to factual information now available, the disturbances at Sharpeville on Monday resulted from a planned demonstration of about 20,000 natives in which demonstrators attacked the Police with assorted weapons including fire-arms. The demonstrators shot first, and the Police were forced to fire in self-defence and avoid even more tragic results. The allegation of the United Nations Afro-Asian group, in requesting a Security Council meeting, that the demonstrators were unarmed and peaceful is therefore completely untrue . . .

Afterwards the South African Government appointed a one-man judicial commission to make an inquiry into the shooting at Sharpeville. Mr. Justice Vessels was named as Commissioner. The Commission was appointed by the Governor General and instructed to inquire and report into the events which had taken place at Vanderbyl Park, Evaton, Vereeniging and Sharpeville on the 21st of March, 1960. Mr. Van Rhyn's statement was in fact not borne out by the evidence placed before the Commission by the attorney general of the Orange Free State, who appeared on behalf of the government. Counsel and attorneys who had been instructed by me appeared at this inquiry, cross-examined certain witnesses and made a series of submissions to the Commission on my behalf and on behalf of the dependents in June 1960. Much of what occurred at the Commission appears in my account of the events at Sharpeville, but certain aspects of the evidence require further comment.

I

THE POLICE EVIDENCE

The first question which deserves comment is the question of the police evidence. I cannot do better than to quote extensively from my Counsel's argument:

Some of the police evidence may be mere exaggeration born of prejudice towards and ignorance of the Africans whom they saw at Sharpeville, or even of inexperience and nervousness . . . Regrettably, however, much of the police evidence about the crowd can only be described as untruthful — as a deliberate and, one is driven to say, a concerted attempt to mislead the Commissioner about the state of the crowd, and to provide some sort of justification for the tragedy which later ensued.

Firstly, the police evidence is completely contradicted by the absence of defensive preparations by the police against attack. If this was a dangerous crowd, the inactivity of the police and the absence of defensive measures are completely inexplicable. The officers and N.C.O.s in charge were experienced men. The only explanation of their failure to take any measures, defensive or offensive, is that there was nothing in the behaviour of the crowd to warrant such measures. All the police did was to ask certain Africans who were inside the fence to tell the crowd to stand back from the fence, which the crowd apparently did when they were so requested.

Secondly, the police evidence is contradicted by the fact that there was no attack on the police before the arrival of the Saracens, either by the crowd as a whole or even by any wild or excitable individuals. The gates were not locked and the fence was a minor obstacle. There was no line of armed police-men and no line of Saracens; yet there was no attack. It is not likely that this crowd, having neglected its opportunities for five hours, decided to make an attack on a line of armed rifle-men and Sten-gunners and in the teeth of four Browning machine guns.

Thirdly, the details of the police evidence of the riotous be-haviour of the crowd do not withstand the simplest critical analysis. Throughout the record the theme is constantly repeated that the crowd was riotous and aggressive and took up a threatening attitude. But what does the evidence amount to? There were shouts of "Afrika," there were thumbs-up signs, and there was the singing of songs. There was shouting, apparently of words or slogans, the meaning of which the police did not understand and did not try to ascertain. A few policemen say that they heard shouts of "Cato Manor" and "police dogs" by some unidentified individuals; but it is not easy to be sure that during the singing and shouting of slogans they correctly heard these remarks; nor did these remarks appear to have been general. No doubt the crowd was noisy. No doubt the crowd was shouting political slogans. But the real crux of the police complaint about the crowd seems to be that the crowd were lacking in that respect and humility which the police apparently expect from their African fellow-citizens. There was, of course, a little police evidence that some of the crowd were waving sticks . . . Moreover, one is again reminded of the fact that this allegedly riotous crowd allowed the police vehicles to enter the Police Station grounds unmolested: no policeman was injured and no police vehicle was damaged. The police evidence is also contradicted by a circumstance to which the police themselves deposed, namely, that a considerable part of the crowd was only at the Police Station by reason of intimidation . . . The police evidence on this point suggests that there were many members of the crowd who had no particular determination to remain at the Police Station and who might even have been glad to get away.

Fourthly, the police evidence is contradicted by the expe-

rience of at least three white men who passed among or
through the crowd at one o'clock or shortly after one o'clock,
namely, Berry — the *Drum* photographer, Hoek — the *Rand
Daily Mail* photographer, and Labuschagne — the superintendent of the Sharpeville Township. Berry walked through
the crowd to the fence. He had no difficulty in getting through
and he met with no hostility. The crowd seemed to him to be
friendly. Hoek did not get out of his car, but he stopped
among the crowd near the Police Station. He thought the
crowd was noisy and excitable but he saw no signs of hostility.
These men, of course, were not policemen, nor was Labuschagne, but Labuschagne was the personification of officialdom
and authority. It was he who, as Superintendent, was responsible for the practical application of the pass laws, for it was
he, or his colleagues in his department, who had to decide
whether any African might enter or must leave the township.
He had been standing quietly for an hour or more with Captain Coetzee's men, but at about one o'clock he decided to
leave them and to enter the Police Station. He walked through
the crowd and climbed over the fence. He met with no hostility; on the contrary, he was greeted in a friendly manner and
chatted with members of the crowd. Moreover, Sergeant Nkosi,
the uniformed charge office sergeant at Sharpeville Police Station, went off duty shortly after 1.0 P.M. He left the Police
Station by the south gate and walked alone through the crowd.
He was not molested in any way.

Fifthly, the police evidence about the crowd is completely
inconsistent with the Press photographs which have been placed
before the commission. Berry's photographs show police vehicles arriving. They show the crowd near the fence and at the
fence itself on both the southern and the western sides. The
pictures speak for themselves. The crowd is not a riotous or
an angry crowd . . . The same can be said of the photographs
taken by Hoek. Some people are trying to see over the heads
of those in front of them; some are strolling about; some are
sitting on the pavement. The photographs taken by the
photographers of the *Golden City Post* and the *Star*, which
were obtained by the Commissioner and are in his possession,

clearly show the scene as the Saracens and other vehicles drove towards the Police Station . . . the vehicles have a clear passage. There is no sign of aggression or riotous behaviour. Most important of all, these pictures show an unarmed crowd . . . One does not see sticks being brandished at the police: indeed, there seem to be many more umbrellas than sticks . . . There seem to be many women and children in the crowd. Above all the crowd depicted in these photographs is not a fanatical crowd or a frenzied crowd. These are not people who have come to commit murder, still less suicide, in a desperate unarmed attack against the tremendous firing power of the police.

Small wonder is it that learned Counsel added,

In these circumstances one must unfortunately conclude that not the slightest credence can be given to the account by the police of riotous behaviour during the morning. Certainly the evidence of the African witnesses cannot be rejected. All that can be said is that it was a large crowd and was making a certain amount of noise.

II

THE SITUATION BEFORE THE SHOOTING

What was the situation before the shooting?

I have already referred to Lieutenant Colonel Pienaar's evidence on this. After some confusion, his men were assembled in single line facing the west side entrance, much closer to the entrance than to the Police Station buildings. This line consisted of about seventy white police; the remainder were apparently standing somewhere behind them. As we have seen, sometime after these men were drawn up, Lieutenant Colonel Pienaar ordered his men to load five rounds, though he knew that in fact many of them had already loaded with the full number of rounds, and during the half hour before the shooting, the police made several arrests and brought in two men from the crowd.

From the photographs taken at the time it is clear that the crowd was pressed fairly closely against the fence. There can be no doubt that there was some pressure on the fence. The photographs show people leaning against it in order to look over it and along it. It does not appear that they were deliberately attempting to damage it. Rather, the pressure on it was simply the natural result of a large number of people standing close to it and in some cases being pushed from behind by those who wished to get a better view of what was going on inside. In any case there were so many easier ways of getting into the Police Station than by pushing down the fence. Certainly the fence remained intact.

Consequently it is clear that, right up to the time of the shooting, the fence was standing as a barrier between the crowd and the police. It was not an insuperable barrier, but the important point is that the police were dealing with the crowd behind an obstacle. Further, it has to be remembered that this crowd was unarmed. Truly the police alleged that, after the shooting, a variety of weapons were left behind. Indeed they were shown to the Commissioner. But there was no evidence where they were found, when they were found or who collected them. And the collection of weapons itself was not impressive: about a dozen sticks, one knobkerrie, two or three hatchets or picks, and about ten pieces of iron. There were also two colored umbrellas and a bicycle pump in working order!

Although some of the police said that the crowd became more noisy during the half hour before the shooting, there was no evidence that its mood was very different from what it had previously been. A number of witnesses said that the crowd became angry when the arrests were made, and it was almost immediately after the last arrest that the firing began. But more important than the statements of witnesses is the fact that twice Colonel Spengler went down to the main gate and opened it in order to bring in a man, and the gate was closed again without any difficulty. It is surely obvious that the crowd was neither threatening nor dangerous.

III

THE SHOOTING BY THE POLICE

The shooting started with a few individual shots, and then a full volley. It did not stop until seven hundred rounds had been fired and the whole crowd dispersed. Lieutenant Colonel Pienaar said firmly that he gave no order to fire. Some of the constables alleged that they heard someone in their ranks say "Shoot," but all the officers and N.C.O.s who gave evidence denied having given any order to shoot. Some of the Africans outside the fence said that they did hear a policeman shout "Shoot" in Afrikaans. It appears from this that somebody who had no authority to give a command did so. In any event, the majority of the policemen who gave evidence said that they fired for other reasons. Some claimed that they fired on their own responsibility when stones were thrown: others said that on hearing shots from elsewhere in the line they assumed that an order to fire had been given. Some, to their credit, did not fire at all. In this category were most of the head constables and sergeants. The inference is that the more experienced and steadier men saw no reason for firing at that stage.

Those who did fire gave four main reasons to justify their action, each of which must be examined in turn.

(i) *They heard shots from the crowd.* Certainly some of the police declared that just before the shooting they heard one or two dull reports from somewhere outside the fence, which sounded like shots fired from a revolver or a small-bore rifle. But Lieutenant Colonel Pienaar said that he was not sure that these reports were revolver shots. Neither he nor anyone else saw anyone in the crowd with a firearm. He agreed that it would be quite wrong to say that the crowd opened fire on the police. Counsel commented, "It is submitted that the police could not genuinely believe that they were being fired on by the crowd."

(ii) *The crowd was rushing the fence.* It is difficult to understand how this can be alleged, for the crowd had been close to the fence all the morning. The most that could be obtained from the police evidence was the allegation of a vague movement of some of the crowd. When pressed, police witnesses said that they did not fire because the fence was being broken down, or even because the crowd was launching an attack, but because they feared that the fence might collapse.

(iii) *The crowd was throwing stones at the police.* Nearly all the police witnesses claim that this happened. On the other hand most of the African witnesses denied that stones were thrown. One of them did see a few stones thrown by children, and another *heard* that some stones had been thrown by children. Counsel submitted that in fact there were only a few stones thrown by children and that the crowd certainly did not stone the police.

(iv) *The mob was rushing in on them through the double gate.* It appears from the evidence of Africans that there was no inrush or attack through the gate. Rather, the probability is that there was some movement of the crowd at the gate but that it was an involuntary movement and not a deliberate incursion. Counsel pointed out that it was difficult for the police to support this contention as they could not explain "what had happened to the Africans who were alleged to have run in. It must be remembered that the line of policemen was only a few paces from the fence. If the gate was the point of attack and a large crowd had rushed in one would have expected some of them to be shot. Yet every policeman agrees that there were no bodies inside the fence, or even in the gateway; nor was any blood seen inside or in the gateway; nor was any weapon or piece of clothing found there. Nor were any dead or wounded found even outside the gate."

IV

THE CONDUCT OF THE POLICE

Was the conduct of the police justifiable? Counsel, on my behalf, placed before the court not only the Standing Orders for the South African Police on the use of arms and Queen's Regulations for the Army, but also an extract from Parliamentary Debates from the House of Commons for July 8, 1920. Mr. Winston Churchill in that debate set out a number of principles which should guide an officer in whose charge there are police or troops, when such an officer has the duty of maintaining public law and order. Mr. Churchill asks:

Is the crowd attacking anything or anybody? Surely that is the question. Are they trying to force their way forward to the attack of some building or some cordon of troops or police, or are they attempting to attack some band of persons or some individual who has excited their hostility? Is the crowd attacking? That is the first question which would naturally arise. The second question is this: Is the crowd armed? That is surely another great simple fundamental question. By armed I mean armed with lethal weapons . . . Armed men are in a category absolutely different from unarmed men. An unarmed crowd stands in a totally different position from an armed crowd.

Mr. Churchill went on to say:

But there is another test which is not quite so simple, but which nevertheless has often served as a good guide. I mean the doctrine that no more force should be used than is necessary to secure compliance with the law . . . [An officer] should confine himself to a limited and definite objective, that is to say, to preventing a crowd doing something which they ought not to do, or to compelling them to do something which they ought to do.

Mr. Churchill concluded by saying:

If there are guides of a positive character, there is surely one guide which we can offer them of a negative character. There is surely one general prohibition which we can make. I mean a prohibition against what is called "frightfulness." What I mean by frightfulness is the inflicting of great slaughter or massacre upon a particular crowd of people, with the intention of terrorising not merely the rest of the crowd, but the whole district or the whole country.

The conduct of the police has been analyzed in the light of the great principles enunciated in this passage, and I have come to the conclusion that not only does the conduct of the police fall far short of these tests, but that the duration and the savage brutality of the firing at Sharpeville was frightful in the full sense of Sir Winston Churchill's definition. And so, in answer to the first question: Was the crowd attacking, killing, or seriously injuring any person; were they destroying or doing serious damage to valuable property, or did they show a manifest intention of doing serious damage to valuable property; in short, was the crowd attacking? there can only be one answer, and that is—no.

Was the crowd ever ordered to disperse and was it ever told that unless it dispersed force would be used? The answer is no.

It is interesting to note that in the last century it has never happened before in any civilized country in the world that a large contingent of police, armed not only with service revolvers and service rifles, but also with Sten guns, has fired into a crowd without first giving an order to disperse and a warning that force would be used.

The police certainly failed to observe the principles I have quoted. They also failed to observe their own standing orders. Regulation 741 of the Standing Orders of the South African Police provides that "firing upon the people is a measure which should never be resorted to until every other means shall have failed to ensure the preservation of peace and good order." As far as I can see, not one of the police officers present ever attempted to find out from the crowd who were its leaders, nor, with the exception of Captain Brummer, did any police officer ever attempt to speak to the crowd or its leaders, or to persuade its leaders to tell the crowd to go home. Lieutenant Colonel Pienaar had, earlier that day, used this method with success at Dube. He says, inexplicably, that at Sharpeville he would not have dealt directly with the leaders of the crowd because, "from past experience it is generally, in most cases, useless." It is fair to say that the South African Police could not point to any measures taken by them to ensure the preservation of peace and good order before they fired.

Another such standing order requires an officer in command of armed policemen to exercise the utmost forbearance and humane discretion. Any policeman who wishes to exercise discretion must take the trouble to ascertain all the relevant facts of an emergency in order to place himself in a position to do this. Lieutenant Colonel Pienaar arrived at Sharpeville under an erroneous impression, and when he got there he did nothing to verify the information which he had received. What is more remarkable, he failed to discuss the situation with the officers who were already at the Police Station; namely, Captain Theron and Captain Brummer. Lieutenant Colonel Pienaar not only did not know how many men he had under his command, but he did not know what armaments he had at his disposal. By deploying a large number of armed policemen in a single line as he did, and failing to make proper inquiries, Lieutenant Colonel Pienaar made it impossible to exercise the humane discretion with which he was entrusted in terms of standing orders.

Another standing order provides that an officer in command of armed policemen must give all his attention to the supervision of the men acting under his orders and must guard against the slightest misuse by his men of their arms. To this end, he must ensure that he deploys his men in such a way that his comments can be communicated to them in all the circumstances of the emergency. It would seem that where a senior officer, as at Sharpeville, has under his command an armed force which is the equivalent of a company of infantry, it is absolutely necessary that he should divide them into sections under the command of his officers and N.C.O.s in order that he may exercise proper command.

Counsel, in the argument, said:

> The deployment of these police, if such it may be called, was not that of a body of men whose purpose was to defend themselves or their station against imminent attack; it more closely resembled that of a firing squad, save that a firing squad

normally consists of a few men in proper control. Lieutenant Colonel Pienaar's line was designed to bring the maximum firing power to bear upon the crowd, instead of the minimum fire power necessary as is required by Standing Orders. Lieutenant Colonel Pienaar should have known that Standing Orders provide that no greater number of men should fire than is absolutely necessary. He would also have known that he must give a deliberate word of command to fire a specific number of rounds, and that the firing ought to be at the leaders of the riot or at the assailants of the force, and that the firing must not be indiscriminate. The answer to the question, "Did Lieutenant Colonel Pienaar observe Standing Orders?" is clearly — no. Standing Orders provide that, where a senior officer is present, the police under his command may not open fire except by a regular word of command.

For what the police did at Sharpeville, a heavy burden of guilt lies not only upon Lieutenant Colonel Pienaar, for his failure to control and superintend his men, but also upon the individual policemen who fired. Standing orders also provide that the police must exercise great care that in firing they merely wound or maim their target and do not kill: at Sharpeville, the police fired recklessly and indiscriminately into an unarmed crowd which was not attacking them. They killed sixty-nine people and no justification or even extenuation can be found for such conduct. Standing orders provide that no shot must be fired after the necessity for firing has ceased. At Sharpeville, the police went on firing into the back of the crowd long after it had turned and begun to flee from the scene. They fired their automatic weapons in tremendous and devastating bursts, and the only problem is to find suitable words of condemnation for conduct of such enormity.

Counsel said in argument:

The names of some of the individual policemen who per-
petrated these dreadful deeds are known. They have shown
themselves unfit to be entrusted with firearms of any kind, let
alone highly dangerous automatic weapons. Apart from any
other steps that may be taken against them, it is to be hoped
that none of them will again be let loose upon the public with
firearms in their possession.

But it is upon Lieutenant Colonel Pienaar's shoulders that
responsibility for this tragedy must most immediately lie, for
once the shooting had started he and his officers seemed to be
quite unable to stop it. I quote the following passages from his
evidence:

Apart from the fact that your order was to load five
rounds, had you no means whatsoever of ensuring that the
firing would stop as soon as it was no longer necessary? — Only
by word of mouth — command.

That is not a very good idea in a noisy place with a line of
men strung over a long distance, is it? — No it is not.

In fact, it is useless, isn't it, in that situation? — I would
not say it is useless. We stopped the fire very soon.

Some of the men, you had reason to believe, would have had
full magazines? — I had reason to believe that; I can't say that
it was so.

You also knew that some of the men had Sten guns? — Yes.

Which, of course, carries on? — Yes.

Ability to stop the shooting if it began was vitally necessary
in the interests of humanity, was it not? — Yes.

But you had no effective arrangement whereby you could
stop the shooting once it had started? — Not with press button
precision.

Not with any sort of precision? — Right.

In fact, you told us yesterday you really left it to the
discretion of your men to stop when they thought it appro-
pirate? — Under these circumstances, if a command became
impossible, they must use their own discretion.

Do you suggest there is no way of doing this sort of thing?
There is no way of . . . ?
Of making arrangements so that you can stop fire when
necessary? — If I had had the time, I could have made different
arrangements.

The most devastating answer which was given by any policeman at the inquiry was given by Lieutenant Colonel Pienaar
when he was asked this question, "Do you think you have
learned any useful lesson from the evidence in Sharpeville?"
He said, "Well we may get better equipment."

V

THE POLICE AND AFRICANS

The tragic story of the events at Sharpeville that morning is
only too clear an indication of the attitude that the police in
South Africa so frequently adopt towards Africans. This attitude was expressed in much of the police evidence at the Commission of Enquiry, for it revealed that when the police are
faced with a crowd of Africans they often regard them, not
as fellow citizens whom it is their duty to protect and help, but
as potential enemies. This may be partly due to prejudice; but
it is much more the result of hatred, contempt and fear. Africans are regarded not as persons but as a "mob" which only
understands the use of force. It became apparent in the police
evidence, as Counsel pointed out, that many of the police expected unquestioning deference from Africans, and when they
did not get it at Sharpeville they interpreted this as riot and
rebellion. There was no real attempt to communicate with the
crowd.

If the crowd had been white, the police would certainly have
tried to make contact with their leaders. They would have

attempted to find out what the crowd wanted and why they were there. If they had wanted them to disperse they would have found some means of telling them to go away. But at Sharpeville, apart from Lieutenant Visser's conversation with Tsolo, and possibly the activities of Lieutenant Colonel Spengler, no attempt was made to get in contact with people in the crowd. Although the crowd was there for some hours, no effort was made to get one of the African police to speak to them in their own language. Why? Surely because it never occurred to the police either to negotiate with Africans or to persuade them to leave. This attitude of hostility and even contempt was further borne out by the free use of the word "tsotsi" by the police as applied to young Africans: the word means a young criminal, hooligan or vagabond. Again, there is the case of the policeman who equipped himself with a sjambok. No policeman would dare to carry a sjambok when faced with a white crowd. Yet no police officer apparently reprimanded him for what was admittedly irregular conduct. In this connection perhaps the most revealing piece of evidence was Lieutenant Colonel Pienaar's statement that "the Native mentality does not allow them to gather for a peaceful demonstration. For them to gather means violence." Such a statement shows a remarkable combination of ignorance and racial prejudice. Coming as it did from a police officer with over thirty years' experience in the force, it probably revealed more about the attitude of many policemen towards Africans than any other single piece of evidence.

All this is underlined by the attitude of some of the police present at Sharpeville after the shooting had taken place, distasteful as it is to refer to it. African witnesses who dealt with statements by policemen after the shooting alleged that some of them were either indifferent or callous. It appears that, apart from supervision by officers, the only persons who took direct action to aid the wounded and remove the dead bodies were either civilians or non-white policemen. There is no evidence that white police themselves rendered aid to the wounded.

This is not to suggest that all white members of the South African Police Force are cruel or callous. Many of them were no doubt shocked by what had happened. But it does emphasize how far they are cut off from any real sympathy with or understanding of Africans. All this has been exemplified by the absence of any official expression of regret from the Police Force for the tragic happening at Sharpeville, either during the Commission of Enquiry or at any other time.

Yet, when all this has been recorded, we come back once again to the fact that this attitude of the police towards Africans has been shaped to no small degree by the South African Government, which has laid on them the almost intolerable burden of administering the mass of repressive legislation of the last ten years. One of the gravest indictments that can be brought against this government is that it has charged the police with fulfilling a task that becomes increasingly difficult to achieve. Few police forces anywhere in the world have a more unenviable task.

As the years pass it is becoming more plain that the worst effects of the present policies are going to fall upon the white minority, who are responsible for a succession of laws which cause much needless suffering and wanton injustice. Already this is beginning to sap the vitality and blunt the moral sense of some of the white people. That I am persuaded is the reason why Counsel at the Sharpeville inquiry felt compelled to draw the attention of the Commissioner to the many instances of police witnesses attempting to mislead him. Counsel alleged that "on a number of occasions members of the police had fabricated evidence or had concealed facts from the Commissioner." As evidence of this concealment he instanced that, despite questions put to the police by Counsel and by the Commissioner, as well as investigation by detectives, no policeman would admit either to having fired the first shot or to having shouted "Shoot." Further, he pointed out that police witnesses had denied that there were any police standing on the Saracens during the shooting. It was only after the photographs of the scene had been produced that the truth emerged. All this illustrates only too vividly the fact that human beings cannot administer unjust laws without serious consequences to themselves.

Mr. Winston Churchill in concluding his address to the British House of Commons called upon members to remember the words of Macaulay, "And then was seen what we believe to be the most frightful of all spectacles, the strength of civilisation without its mercy." Can any more apt description of the events at Sharpeville be found than this?

VI

FINAL CONCLUSIONS OF COUNSEL APPEARING ON BEHALF OF THE BISHOP OF JOHANNESBURG

The truth is that the police at Sharpeville disregarded both the letter and the spirit of their own Standing Orders and disobeyed the law of the land.

The officers made no attempt to persuade the crowd by non-violent means to disperse.

The officers failed to *order* the crowd to disperse.

The officers failed to warn the crowd that if they did not disperse force would be used.

The officers made no attempt to use any form of force less drastic than firearms.

The officers failed to supervise and control the men under their command.

The officers took no steps to ensure that if shooting started it would be limited and controlled and could be stopped.

The constables started shooting without receiving an order to do so.

Many of the constables shot to kill not merely to wound.

They did kill sixty-nine people including eight women and ten children.

The shooting was indiscriminate, and continued long after the crowd had turned and fled.

The 180 wounded included thirty-one women and nineteen children.

There was no justification for the police to open fire on the crowd and therefore no justification for the conduct of the police.

CONCLUSION

THE IMMEDIATE CONSEQUENCE of the shooting at Sharpeville was the declaration of a State of Emergency and the publication of Emergency Regulations. By these regulations magistrates and commissioned officers were empowered to prohibit gatherings or processions unless these were being held for the purpose of religious worship, weddings, funerals, meetings of statutory bodies and industrial councils, or for theatrical or cinematographic entertainment. These officials were further empowered to arrest and detain any person with or without a warrant if it were considered by them to be in the interests of public safety or order to do so. Those so arrested could be detained if it was deemed necessary until the termination of the State of Emergency. No charge needed to be preferred against them and it was not necessary for them to be brought to trial. Some 1900 people of all races were actually held in this way, including two of the attorneys engaged by me to prepare submissions for the Sharpeville Commission of Enquiry. Some three to four months later practically all these people were released, without any charge having been brought against them. A further 20,000 Africans were detained on the allegation that they were idlers.

At the same time that the Emergency Regulations were promulgated, both the African National Congress and the Pan-

African Congress were banned. The result of this ban is that the Africans have been deprived of any legitimate political organization through which they may express their opposition to government policy. Further, the shooting at Sharpeville means the end of peaceful African demonstrations as an expression of opposition, because no African dares take part in such demonstrations for fear of being shot by South African police. This in itself is most serious, for the Africans are thereby deprived of the only ways in which in the past they have been able to draw attention to their grievances.

Although Sharpeville was not an isolated incident in recent South African history it focused the attention of millions of people all over the world upon the fears and frustrations, the resentment and hatred engendered by the implementation of the policy of apartheid. Sharpeville was only one of the many tragic consequences of the desperate endeavor to preserve what is called "white civilization." According to the exponents of apartheid, this civilization can only be preserved by taking every step possible to ensure that all political and economic power is kept in the hands of the white minority.

Not by any means all white people in South Africa support this fanatical racial sectarianism. Not even all Afrikaners stand behind the implementation of apartheid. It does a grave injustice to the Afrikaans-speaking South Africans to identify them all with the policies of those now in power in South Africa. The majority of white people have supported these policies largely because they have believed that there is no other way of preserving their own way of life; and it has to be remembered that, after the tragedy at Sharpeville, apart from the immediate financial aid cabled by Christian Action in London, it was white people in Johannesburg and the neighboring towns who supplied food, clothing and money for the victims of the outrage. But to those in power, nothing must be allowed to disturb the privileged position of the white minority. White supremacy must be maintained, and those of other races must accept at the hands of the white group just what that group judges is best for them.

Today the word *apartheid* is rarely used to describe the policy of the South African Government. Normally it is now presented to the world as separate development, with the implication that it is only as each racial group is allowed to develop along its own lines that it will be able to fulfil the destiny that God intends it to fulfil. Superficially, this may sound very reasonable — until we remember that, by its very nature, separate development within a community usually involves inequality. Even if this were not inevitably the case, it must be so in South Africa, for this separate development has to take place within the context of, and subordinate to, white supremacy. The result is that, whatever words may be used to describe the policy of apartheid, those in power are in effect claiming that the members of the white group have the right to determine the destiny of all the non-white peoples; a right that belongs alone to God, who has given to all men their destiny. In the last resort, even if they do not put it into words, they are claiming that they are the agents of God's will for all the peoples in South Africa. Separate development must degrade the non-whites, for it carries with it by implication belief in their inferiority. Little wonder is it that those who champion apartheid are far from convincing in their efforts to explain the mass of discriminatory legislation that has been enacted during the last decade.

For the Christian more still has to be said, because apartheid is an offense against the Gospel and a denial of the mystery of our redemption in Jesus Christ; as such it must be opposed.

In the end, the opposition of Christians to apartheid rests not on political or economic grounds, but on the conviction that apartheid is a complete negation of the teaching of the New Testament and the traditional practice of the Church. It is not merely that apartheid is erroneous: it is a heresy, doing violence to the Christian faith in God and in the nature and destiny of man. It is the Christian belief that, whatever our racial origin may have been, we all share in the same Spirit. Certainly it is unthinkable that within the Church differences of race and color should be allowed to continue to separate Christians from one another.

While Christians retain the color of their skin, their racial origin and their particular cultural background, in Christ and his Church they ought to, and can, experience a unity that is so deep that it transcends all their natural differences. And just because Christians can experience such a unity in Christ, in the fellowship of the Church, they are compelled in the world to do their utmost to remove the fear, suspicion and mistrust which are always threatening to divide men from one another. That is the high calling of Christians. Always they have first to allow the dross of racial pride and false nationalism to be burned up in themselves, and then to seek to live out their unity in Christ in the world. Before it is too late, some better way of fashioning the life of society in South Africa must be found than that which is possible under apartheid. This can only be begun when those in authority are willing and ready to have effective consultation with responsible African, Indian and Colored leaders, so that together they may shape the structure of the South African society of the future. The non-white peoples in South Africa increasingly resent having their lives ordered for them by others, even if they are well ordered. They want to be free to make their own mistakes and to order their lives as they believe they ought to be ordered. In short, they want to live as human beings.

I do not say that such consultation will be easy. Just as it is folly to imagine that the problems which now confront the peoples in South Africa would be resolved once the policy of apartheid is abandoned, so it would be stupid to conclude that all that is needed is to get the leaders of all racial groups to come together for consultation. That in itself grows more difficult as the months pass, and, even if it is achieved, much prejudice and fear will still remain. A great deal of clear thinking will be needed if any way through the present impasse is to be found; and those concerned will have to exercise much patience and forbearance with one another, as well as a willingness to forgive if peoples of such varied languages, traditions and cultures are to be able to learn to live together. Nonetheless, the passing of apartheid would in itself remove many of the present quite unnecessary strains and tensions, and make possible a new beginning in race relationships. At any rate, the Christians in South Africa would again have the chance, at present largely denied them, of demonstrating that the Gospel has the power to unite rather than separate men, in spite of all racial differences.

Sharpeville was a tragedy. But out of that evil event good may yet come if those in South Africa turn from the bitterness of the past, believing that God has some better thing in store for all the peoples of their country than the way of apartheid, which has shown all too clearly that it is a way of death and not of life.

DOCUMENTARY I

Mr. Wentzel/RC.

Col. Lemmer,
Deputy Commissioner of Police,
The Grays,
cor. von Wielligh & Main Streets,
JOHANNESBURG.

22nd March, 1960.

Dear Sir,

We have been instructed by the Bishop of Johannesburg, the Rt. Rev. Ambrose Reeves, to write to you about his interview with you at your office yesterday afternoon.

We are instructed that, through Mr. Unterhalter, who accompanied him, he requested you to make certain arrangements in regard to wounded persons from the Sharpeville Location, who were being attended to at the Baragwanath Hospital. He informed you, that it was thought that these people would be arrested upon their discharge from the Hospital, and that many of them were fearful of being manhandled by the Police, if this should happen. Further some of them, if held in prison while awaiting trial, might need special care because of the injuries they had received.

It was therefore suggested to you that, in all the circumstances of the present situation, it would be in the interests of those persons and of peace and order generally, that they should after they were arrested immediately be admitted to bail at the nearest Police Post by a competent police official.

You replied that this request could not be acceded to. You stated that any offences for which people might be arrested were presently being investigated, and until investigations were completed no question of arrest arose. If people were arrested they could make their request for bail when they appeared before the Court. You discounted entirely any suggestion that members of the Police would, when arresting or after arresting, use any unlawful force towards those persons whom they took into custody.

Yours faithfully,

ROUTLEDGE, DOUGLAS WILSON, AURET & WIMBLE.

Per:

TO BE DELIVERED:

DOCUMENTARY II

ROBERT MAJA, *sworn, states (through Interpreter)*:

Examined by Mr. Kentridge:

Mr. Maja, you are a Minister of the Presbyterian Church of South Africa? — I am.

An ordained Minister? — I am an ordained Minister.

Do you live in Sharpeville? — I do.

And do you have a congregation there? — Yes; I have.

Are there many in your congregation? — Yes, there are.

And do you conduct regular services? — I do.

Do you have a school? — Yes. I have had a school built but it was taken over by the Government.

On March 21 of this year, were you in Sharpeville? — I was.

At about what time did you leave your house on the morning of the 21st? — I am not so sure about the time but I think it was between ten and eleven.

And where did you go? — I went to one Minister, Mr. Voyi who is a Minister of the Anglican Church.

In Sharpeville? — Yes; at Sharpeville.

Did you go to his house? — Yes; I did.

Is his house near to the Police Station? — It is a little distance from there, but not very far.

Would you please examine this photograph and see if you can

point out where the house is? — [Witness indicates.]

His house, then, is to the east of the Police Station and behind the Salvation Army church? — That is correct.

When you arrived at his house, what . . . did you find him home? — I found his wife at home and I enquired from her where he was, and she told me that he had gone to the Police Station.

And did you also go to the Police Station? — Yes. I then passed to look for him at the Police Station.

Did you find a crowd of people at the Police Station? — I found many people in the open, there.

Near the Police Station? — Yes.

Did you find Mr. Voyi? — No; the crowd was too big. I did not find him there.

Did you spend some time there among the crowd? — I did. I walked about amongst the crowd, there, to try and see if I could find him but I could not find him.

Can you tell us what the mood of the crowd was at that time? — They were happy.

Did the crowd seem to you to be aggressive? — No.

Or hostile towards the police? — There was nothing indicating fighting.

You did not see any weapons carried by members of the crowd? — Not a single one.

At the time you were there at the Police Station amongst the crowd, did you notice any aeroplanes flying over? — Yes; they did. A few would come and thereafter a few again, and so forth.

Did they dive low over the crowd? — Yes; they did. There were youngsters that were throwing their hats at these aeroplanes — "Hoorah! Hoorah!" — flinging their hats up.

Were these young people who were doing that? — Young boys. And how did you interpret that gesture of throwing their hats into the air and shouting "Hoorah!"? — They were enjoying it.

After a time, did you leave? — Yes; I did, to look for Mr. Voyi.

Did you return to his house? — Yes; I did and I asked his wife to make me a cup of tea.

And did you have tea there? — Yes; I had some tea there: myself and Mr. Voyi, and Mr. Majola.

Is Mr. Majola also a clergyman? — He is a Minister of the Presbyterian Church of Hama Zimba; that is what the church is called.

Did you stay for some time at Mr. Voyi's house? — Yes; I did.

Were you still there when the shooting broke out? — Yes, I was.

Were you sitting indoors, or outdoors? — We were outside, on the stoep of the garage.

From where you were sitting, was it possible for you to see any part of the crowd around the Police Station? — Yes. I could see the crowd from there but I could not say what was happening.

Could you hear, for instance, singing or shouting from the crowd, from Mr. Voyi's house? — May I explain it this way: these people that were there were not controlled by anyone. You would find a few people, five or six singing; others sing there. They were not under control that they should listen to one saying not to do this or that, whatever is to be done.

Were you still on the verandah when the firing started? — I was at Mr. Voyi's place when the firing . . .

And did you hear it? — Oh, very clearly.

And did you run out of the house? — At first, before I went out, I asked Mr. Voyi that the two of us go there where the shooting takes place, to try and prevent it, putting a stop to it.

Did you go out? — Yes, I did.

Did you cross the field next to the Police Station? — I did.

Did you see anything there? — Such as what?

Well, did you see any bodies? — There were many people lying there; some of them were dead; some of them, their intestines were protruding.

Did you go right up to the Police Station? — No. I did not then, having seen that, go to the Police Station. I tried to render assistance to these injured people.

But how far did you go, when you were going to render assistance; did you walk close to the Police Station? — From body to body.

The Chairman: From which side would you approach the Police Station; would it be along Zwane Street, or on the northern side, that is the side where the shops are? — I was on the shops' side.

Examination continued:

Did you see any of the crowd running while shooting was still going on? — When the first report of the firearms started, then the people started running.

Did you see that? — I did; with my eyes.

Did you see any of them fall? — Yes; I did.

Where? — Before I had got out of Mr. Voyi's house, a woman fell in front of the gate leading to his garage and a youth fell in front of the gates of his yard.

Do you know why they fell? — I went to this woman and I saw that she was bleeding, and I did not take notice thereafter because my eyes were looking further on.

Was she shot? — Yes; she was. She was bleeding.

This place where you saw the woman fall, could you describe it more clearly. Was it in the field? — It was about two yards from Mr. Voyi's gate.

Was it near the Salvation Army church? — No. I am sorry; it was two feet from the gate.

Let's make it clear. Where this woman fell — just think of that place; was it further from the Police Station than the Salvation Army? — Far from the Salvation Army, too; just close to the gate.

Mr. Voyi's house is further from the Police Station than the Salvation Army church? — Yes.

When you went after the shooting to these bodies, did you see any clothing lying about on the ground — hats or shoes? — There were a number of shoes and hats.

Did you see sticks lying about? — None.

Did you render assistance to the wounded? — Every corpse that was lying on that opening — I passed every one of them and I gave some of them water.

Where did you get the water? — When I was at Machiba the people who were down there knew me. They called me by name. They said, "Minister Maja, I am thirsty; I want some water." Some of them said, "Minister Maja, I have been burnt terribly by the sun." I tried by taking their shoes to make a pillow for them to lie on. The wounded, what I could pick up there as far as the clothing was concerned, I tried to cover them with that to protect them against the burning of the sun.

Where did you get the water? — On the other side of the road, at the corner. I saw a woman with a big canned-fruit bottle. I ran to her and I took that bottle from her and I went over into the yard, and there I drew water.

Did you spend some time amongst the wounded, there? — I was the last one to leave after the dead had been removed, and the wounded.

I just want to show you a photograph that was taken after the shooting. Do you see it? — That is me, assisting there.

That is a photograph taken — one of those produced by Mr. Robinson, of the *Rand Daily Mail?*—That is me.

Is that the bottle you are speaking of? — Yes; that is the bottle I was speaking about. [Photograph of R. Maja assisting wounded, Exhibit "TTT," handed in. See Plate 25.]

Now, here is another photograph taken by the photographer of the *Star* after the shooting. Is that you in the photograph? — I am the one in front of them here. I went and fetched an officer — this is the man I referred to; the brains were lying out.

What did you do about that? — Before the ambulance came, I went to all the captains. I said, "I am asking you, if you take that corpse, please remove the brains as well." When the Minister Mahawne came to me before the corpse was removed, it then came to my mind that they had left the brains behind. I went back to the captain that I had spoken to previously. I said, "I asked you to remove the brains." It was then that he called this non-European Policeman and told him to remove the brains from there. [As shown.]

[Photograph showing Bantu constable picking up brains with spade, Exhibit "UUU" handed in.]

That is yourself on the photograph? — That's me.

And is the Rev. Voyi in the photograph? — No, he is not there.

Amongst the people who were dead and injured, did you find anyone you knew? — It is hard to say. I cannot say because at that time I was very busy indeed. I was very energetic to see what was happening, then.

Did you find afterwards, though, when you heard later who had been killed, and who had been wounded, that you knew any of the people? — Some of my congregation were shot dead.

What sort of people were they? — I remember an old man,

Sepampoere: he was an old man.

Was he killed? — Yes; he was killed.

What sort of a man was he? — A very decent man.

Is he the sort of man you would expect to go fighting the police? — No.

Is his widow called Salamina? — It is very hard to get the name unless I refer to the books.

And the other members of your congregation whom you found had been either killed or wounded, were they decent people? — Some of them were youngsters. It is hard to explain how old they were.

And were some adults? — Yes; they were.

In general I would like to ask you about this crowd as it was when you saw it. We have heard mention in this Commission of tsotsis. Would you have described it as a crowd of tsotsis? — No.

The Chairman: I don't think anyone has up to now described the crowd as a crowd of tsotsis.

Examination continued:

Did you notice in general whether the people in the crowd seemed to be ordinary, decent people? — It is hard to say that a person is a tsotsi unless you know his behaviour, or something about him, or his movements.

Well, in that case, I will simply just ask you again: When you saw that crowd, did you see any aggressive behaviour, anything which looked like fighting or an intention to fight? — I have come here to speak and I have said there was nothing amongst the crowd there that I saw. They behaved very well. I went to all these people that were injured and the dead, as I have said and these people looked at me and there was not a single one came and asked me what had happened; they were just looking at me. They looked at me in a manner as if they were going to ask what was happening.

Did they appear surprised? — Very.

I take it that you must have spoken to people in Sharpeville about the shooting? — How?

In general; I'll put it this way: have you heard anything which would explain to you why the shooting took place? — The whole Sharpeville village is surprised, only to say in regard to how they feel about it — they are all surprised as to how the shooting took place; they don't know why.

During the course of that morning, the morning of the 21st, were you at any time asked by the authorities to speak on their behalf to the people? — No.

Do you know whether there was any damage to the houses of the people in Sharpeville as a result of the shooting? — I know about one house, yes. One of my friends' house was struck by two bullets. It is practically out of the Sharpeville village, to the west.

Was he struck when he was in his house? — No; the house was struck.

Whereabouts was this? — That was just outside the Sharpeville village, towards the A.N.E. Church.

Would that be to the west of the Police Station? — Yes.

About how far from the Police Station, would you estimate? — You have to cross many streets before you get to that house.

Have you come across any case of any person being injured by a bullet when he was at home? — I know of one instance where a wife told me that her husband, while lying on the lawn reading a book at his house, was shot in the foot or in the leg.

I want to ask you a final question about the crowd as it was when you were there. Were you able to get any impression

of why they were there, what they were waiting for? — Before
I reply to your question, I would like you to listen to my feelings first. When I was walking amongst those people, there, I
was not taking matters—I was not concerned about the people
there. My main object was looking for Mr. Voyi. I heard it
being said amongst them that there was someone who was
going to speak to them at two o'clock.

No further questions.

*　　*　　*

LECHAEL MUSIBI, *sworn, states (through Interpreter)*:

Examined by Mr. Kentridge:

You are the school-teacher in Sharpeville, are you not? — Yes.
Do you remember the 21st March? — Yes.
On that day, did the children come to school? — [Without
interpreter.] No; they did not come to school.
Did you go to the school? — Yes; I went there.
And what did you do during the morning? — During the morn-
ing, I went there. There were no people there. I only saw
the Principal later on come in and then he also left; and then
I also left.
Did you then go home? — Yes; I went home.
During that morning, did you see people in the streets in
Sharpeville? — Yes; I saw people in the streets.
Did you speak to anyone? — To some I spoke.
Did you hear whether anything was happening that day? —
Yes; I heard.
What did you hear from the people? — I heard that some of
the Pan-African members had organised that the people should
not go to work.

And what were they to do instead? — They had to go to the Police Station and expect the big boss who was going to address them at two o'clock.

Did you go to the Police Station to take part in this? — No; I did not go there.

Now, some time after one o'clock did you leave your house? — Yes; I did leave my house when it was one, or just after one o'clock.

How did you go; on foot? — No. I was cycling.

Where were you cycling to? — I was cycling to school, to go and fetch my books there.

And were you going to see anyone in particular? — No. I was not going to see anyone in particular, but when I came to school I remembered that the keys were with another boy who is in my class, who stays somewhere on the other side of the Location; so I cycled up to him.

And when you cycled there, did you have to pass the Police Station? — Yes; I was to pass the Police Station. After leaving, I had to cycle between the Police Station and the cafés.

And how did you cycle; did you cycle across the field? — Yes; there is a footpath on the right hand side of the Police Station, so I followed that footpath. As I saw the people, I think I turned to the tarred road joining Seeiso Street.

Is that the tarred road that runs in front of the west side of the Police Station and in front of the shops? — That's right.

And when you got to that tarred road, were you still on your bicycle? — Yes; I was still, because there were people in front of me.

And when you got on to that tarred road what happened? — Just when I think I reached the intersection of the roads, I think I was just standing and then the shooting started there. I do not know whether I was shot or the crowd fell on me. I found myself lying flat on my bicycle at that time.

Later on you discovered that you had been shot? — Yes. I discovered after the . . .

In what part of the body were you shot? — I was shot in the left leg.

The Chairman: Below, or above the knee? — Below the knee. So when I . . .

Examination continued:

You have told us how you fell over? — Yes.

Did you remain lying down? — Yes; I remained lying down; I think for a short time or some few seconds the shooting stopped. Then I found that I was lying uncomfortably on the bicycle. I rose. Just when I rose myself, there was another shooting, then I got a better place — I laid myself flat on the ground.

And eventually the shooting stopped completely? — Yes; it stopped completely. When I woke, I wanted to take my bicycle but I thought if I take my bicycle, they will shoot again. So I just proceeded in the direction of the library which is facing the cafés, and then I went on the other side. On the other side one of the school children or so started screaming, "They shot you." So I examined myself only to realise that I was shot in the leg.

At the place where you were shot, did you see any other people falling? — Yes; there were many who fell.

Did they just fall, or were they perhaps shot? — I think they were shot, because they just fell. Most men just dropped down.

At this stage when you were shot, was it near the fence of the Police Station? — I don't think it was near the fence of the Police Station. It might have been — my estimation is poor, because there was a big crowd, there; but I think it was not very, very far from the Police Station. I cannot just make it clearly, whether it was near the Police Station, but I think it was not very far from the Police Station.

Well, can you tell the Commissioner, do you think it was nearer the shops, or nearer the Police Station? — I think I was nearer to the Police Station.

No further questions.

Re-examined by Mr. Kentridge:

Now, you were asked whether people came to take statements from you when you were in the hospital ward. I think you were asked whether anyone had mentioned to you the question of whether people were coming to the Police Station expecting an announcement. Did anyone suggest to you that that is what you should say? — No; not at all.

Did anyone suggest to you that you should say anything? — No one.

My learned friend, the other Advocate, suggested to you that what you said about passing the Police Station was not true. Now, before I ask you a question about that, I had better enquire whether that suggestion to you was made on any information or evidence which the other Advocate has. I don't know whether my learned friend put that suggestion to the witness on information or instructions which he had, that the evidence on this point was not true.

Mr. Claassen: I am not [inaudible].

Re-examination continued:

In that case, I'll just ask you again: You said that you passed the Police Station on your way to the house. Was that true? — Yes; it is true.

Well, in that case all I can do is apologise to you for a humiliating and improper question that was put to you.

The Chairman: . . . That morning, as you were going to

school, you had to cross Seeiso Street? — That's right.

Do you remember, what was the position in Seeiso Street at that time? — There were people as I passed, I saw people down towards the Superintendent's office, right down; there was a crowd of people. It seemed as if they were standing right down there.

Extending right down to the Superintendent's office? — Not too close; just — on this side of the hostel, but in the Location — when I was passing. And there were some people going down, at the time when I was first going to school.

At any time that morning, that is after seven, and before eleven o'clock, did you become aware of any unrest in that particular area, in Seeiso Street and in the area immediately surrounding the hostels? — No; the hostels are too far to be seen by me.

You could not see them? — I could not see them. But on coming back, I think it was between ten-thirty or eleven, I saw the police driving the people upwards.

About what time? — I think it was between ten and eleven; I am not quite sure.

Where was that? — That was just below my place, in Seeiso Street; and then the big crowd was coming up. Then I went home.

I just want you to describe to me. You saw the police chasing the people? — No; the people were retreating and the policemen were coming up.

Were they retreating down Seeiso Street, that is in the direction of where your school is, or were they going the other way, that is towards where the exit is from . . . ? — No; they were retreating up Seeiso — not towards the school, but going past — I think they were coming up towards the school, in the direction of the school, but in Seeiso Street.

I want to know their direction of movement. Were they moving in the direction of say the Municipal Offices, or were they moving away from it? — They were moving away from it.

That is deeper into Sharpeville? — Yes; deeper into the Location.

Did you hear shots being fired at any time that morning? — No; not at all.

Could you perhaps just describe to me again — you can look at Exhibit "C" — the road along which you cycled as you were going to this house which is marked "X5"? You mentioned certain names of streets. I'm afraid I don't know where they are? — [Witness indicates.]

I think you have described that you travelled along one of the streets which lies immediately to the southeast of the school, and parallel to Seeiso Street? — That's right.

And you travelled down, in the direction of the Sharpeville Police Station and from there you then wanted to cross over so as to cross Seeiso Street, to go to the house indicated, X5? — Yes. The third or fourth house.

You have told me that you heard before the Monday that there was going to be some demonstration? — Yes.

— *Adjourned:* 10.45 A.M.
— *Resumed:* 11.15 A.M.

LECHAEL MUSIBI, *still under oath:*

The Chairman: At the adjournment, I think I asked you a question as to what you heard that morning? — Yes.

I want to see if you can help me a little further. You said that you knew before the 21st that there was going to be a demonstration? — That's correct.

I am not concerned with whether you were in sympathy with it or what you thought about it; that does not interest me. What I do want to know from you, is this: When you first heard this matter being discussed, was there any reference to

a date when it would take place? — Yes; I heard it was intended
for Monday.

I think you said you thought you heard that on the Saturday?
— Friday or Saturday.

Did you hear any discussion in Sharpeville before that Friday
or Saturday that at some time in the future there was going
to be a demonstration along these lines, organised by the
P.A.C.? — No.

You did not hear it? — No.

Evidence has been given here of pamphlets which were apparently distributed in the township. Did you yourself receive
or see any of these pamphlets at any time?—No.

Now, the discussion which you said you heard in Seeiso Street
and possibly elsewhere, about a person who was coming to
address the inhabitants on this question of passes, did you hear
it only on one occasion or did it appear to be a general discussion amongst the crowd as they passed you? — Yes, as they
passed me, there were some who said "Where are you going
to?" and I told them "I am going to school." So they said
"There is going to be an address by the Chief Commissioner at
the Police Station." I said "No, I did not hear" and I passed
on.

You say you were on your way to school? — That's right.

What time was that? — It was about — between ten-thirty and
eleven o'clock.

Was that the occasion before the aeroplanes flew over? — That's
right, yes.

At that time, when you heard this discussion, was a time specif-
ically mentioned to you? Did you hear that this person was
going to address the people at two o'clock? — They said about
two o'clock.

And from the discussion which you heard, you say you under-

stood it was going to be the Chief Bantu Commissioner? —
Yes.

When you came round that street from the school, while you
were on your way to this house which I marked "X5," did you
get any impression of the size of the crowd around the Police
Station? — Not exactly; but I saw on my left, as I was passing,
that the crowd was very big and the others were still going to
the Police Station. The others were moving in front of me.

At that time, as you got within hearing distance, can you
describe to me what the mood of the crowd was as you saw it?
You are a teacher; you would be able to describe what you saw?
—The mood of the crowd, as I saw them, was very calm. They
were just idling — as if they were anxious to get to the Police
Station; that is the impression I got.

Did you hear any shouting? — No shouting.

You didn't hear? — I didn't hear that.

Another thing I wanted to ask you, is this: Can you give me
the time that you either left the school or the time that you
went past this Police Station? — I was not very particular about
the time, but I think it was about half past one, when I left
the school.

And did you cycle directly from there up to the point where you
eventually were injured? — Yes.

What happened to you after the shooting had stopped? — I fell
down on my bicycle. When I realised, I was lying flat on my
bicycle. There were some people who had fallen on me, and
others had fallen at my side. After the first shooting, I think
there was an interval of a few seconds, and then I thought all
was over, then I woke up. When I woke up, I tried to walk
away. I was ready to take the bicycle, but shooting started
again and then I lay down flat. It was a better position than
lying on the bicycle. I lay flat, there, then the shooting went

on until it stopped. After it stopped, I thought it was over. Then I stood. When I wanted to take the bicycle, I thought I would be shot so I just proceeded towards the library.

Where is the library? — Just opposite the cafés.

Is it that big building — that big hall? — [Witness indicates on Exhibit "C."]

It is the building immediately to the West of the . . . ? — Of the cafés.

And did you stay there? — No. At the time I did not realise that I was shot, but when I got to the library I saw some people who were very interested and I think one of the schoolgirls or so shouted, "Look. He's shot!" Then I started examining myself; when I looked, as I saw this child looking down there— I looked in front and I was shot in the leg. Then I got into the yard just opposite the library and found some of the people there who were shot, as well as some of the women. The women were screaming there. One was shot in the pelvis. I walked a little and I saw cars passing. I tried to stop them — I think there were three, and then the fourth one, I think, I got into that one. I think just before we reached the Superintendent's office, we then saw traffic cops there. The driver was afraid of them and he stopped and we alighted. Then we walked a little way to the bus stop. We saw a car, there, standing. We learned afterwards that those people were going about, there, so we begged them to take us to the hospital; and then I was taken to the hospital. That is when we left.

You weren't there when the ambulances came? — When the ambulances came, I was already in the hospital — when they started leaving. I saw some of the ambulances passing, going to Sharpeville. I was already there.

Which hospital did you go to? — Vereeniging Hospital.

Do you remember when you got to the Vereeniging Hospital?

I suppose you did not look at the time, then? — No; I don't know. But I think it was not very long after the shooting.

The shooting, so far as you remember it, did it start with single shots or was there firing from a whole lot of rifles, all at once? — It seemed to be simultaneous.

You did not hear any single shots? — No.

Then you say there was a break of a few seconds? — Yes.

How long do you estimate that first burst of shooting lasted? — Well, it should have been about half a minute, the first one.

Is it your impression that it was short, or long? — My impression is simply this, it was too long.

Yes, I know, too long; but did it take a short time, the first burst, or . . . ? — The first burst was longer than the second burst.

And the second burst, how long do you think that took; less than half a minute? — Yes; less than half a minute.

Cross-examination by Mr. Louw (translated from Afrikaans):

Did you hear much singing there? — Yes they were singing.

What were they singing? — Christian songs.

Do you go to church? — Yes.

Are they songs which you sing in church, or do you sing them outside the church? — They are the songs which are in the hymn books.

What other songs did you sing? — They were singing "Abide with Me."

Did you see Molefi there? — Molefi who?

Peter Molefi. — I do not know the man.

No further questions.

*   *   *

JOSHUA MOTHA, *sworn, states (through Interpreter)*:

Examined by Mr. Kentridge:

Joshua, you are a Sharpeville man, are you? — I am.

And you are a bus driver? — Yes; I am.

Are you one of the drivers who drive the buses between Sharpeville and Vereeniging? — Yes; I am.

Do you remember the night before the 21st March, that is the night before the shooting; do you remember that night? — I do.

Did anything happen to you during that night? — Yes.

What was it? — Some people came along and woke me during the night.

At your house? — At my house.

And what did they do? — They said that we had to go along with them, out of the Location.

Did you know those people? — I only knew some of them by sight; others I did not know.

And did they say why you had to go out of the Location? — They said we were going to go out and fetch some buses. They said that they did not want any transport to be so that the passengers are people to be conveyed.

Were you willing to go with them? — I did not want to go, but I thought that should I not go along with them, they might injure me, or cause me some injury.

And did you go with them? — I did.

Where did they take you? — To some trees, towards the Vanderbijl side.

And how long did they keep you there? — We sat there and then it became light; until the sun came up.

And then, what happened? — It was then said that we had to

go to the Police Station to report why we did not go to work.
And did you do that? —We went there.
And did you report at the Police Station? — We did.
Were there other bus drivers with you? — Yes.
And what happened at the Police Station? Did you report to
somebody? — Yes; we reported to a non-European sergeant
who was there.
And did he tell you to do anything? — No.
Did you then go home? — From there, I went home.
Did you stay at home for some time? — I was about ten min-
utes at home, and I asked my wife to give me some food. As she
was preparing the food, some other people came. It appeared
to be young people. They said to me, "Oh, you are at home;
don't you know that all the people are required at the Police
Station?" I said, "I have just come from there. I have come to
get something to eat!" I also said, "You know that I left during
the night and I slept in the veld. I am hungry." They said,
"No, let us go; all the men are required at the Police Station."
They also said that the man who remains at home and does not
go there, might meet with an accident or something serious.
So did you go to the Police Station? — I did.
And were there many people at the Police Station when you
got there? — When I got there, there were many people.
Have you any idea what time it was? — I do not remember
clearly as to what the time was.
Was it before the aeroplanes came over, or after? — Just after
we had got to the Police Station, the aeroplanes came.
And where did you stand at the Police Station? — I went and
stood on the western side of the big gate.
Were you near the big gate? — I was near, but not very near.
Were you near the fence? — On account of many people that
were close to the fence, I could not get there.

Do you know a man called Tsolo? — Yes.

Did you see him there? — I did.

Did you hear him speak? — At the time the aeroplanes were going over the Police Station, backwards and forwards, and I saw him, Tsolo, at that time, speaking to a European at the entrance to the Police Station. From there, he came to us. He then said to us that it had been said that we will get the reply at two o'clock. He then returned. When he came back from there, he then said, "It is said that we have to go to the football grounds." He came out at the gate, and he said, "Follow me; we are going to the football grounds." The people then said "Now! But it may be that they want these aeroplanes to collide with us. We are afraid to go to the football grounds." If anything was to be said, we would listen to what was to be said from here, where we stand, where we are.

Did Tsolo say anything about what time something might be said? — Yes; he said at about two o'clock.

Did he just say it himself, or did he indicate that someone had told him that? — He said it was said.

And did he say who had said it to him? — No. I only heard him saying "It is being said," but I did not hear who had told him that or said that to him.

Did you wait there all the time, or did you go home? — I tried to go home. As I was proceeding towards home down Zwane Street, to turn off into the street that leads to my home, a bit lower down in Zwane Street there were some police. Not far this side of where the police were, I turned to the right, into some small street which was on my right. I had not gone far when these young men, the tsotsis, came along and said to me, "Where are you going to?" I said, "No, I am just looking for a lavatory." They said, "Well, there are any amount of lavatories; it does not matter what yard you enter. You people want to

run away when you do this." They also said that they did not
want to cause any trouble, or make any trouble. They said,
"But if you people run away and go to your homes, you might
be injured." I then came back.

Did you then go near the gate? — I came back and I again went
and stood near the gate.

At various times, did you see Saracens and other police cars
go into the grounds? — Yes.

Do you remember when the last car went into the police
grounds? — I don't know, because as the vehicles were entering
the police yard, I went to the café. I do not know when the
last vehicle went in.

And then did you come back from the cafés? — I went to the
cafés, and I had a cold drink. I came back. I had not gone
far from the cafés, I shall say between the cafés and the charge
office, when I met a person who I knew by the name of George
Mtshale and I stood and spoke to him. As I was standing there,
speaking to this man, three small vehicles came from the Town
Hall side. These vehicles also came and entered the police
premises. We heard someone say, "Well, here is the big man;
here is the big man," and we all thought that was the man.
We all drew nearer.

Did you also draw nearer? — I did.

When you drew nearer, did you see anything after that; did
you see anything happen near the gate? — I did not see with
my own eyes what was happening at the gate, but I saw a woman
who was limping and she said she — one of the vehicles that
had entered had collided with her. We stood there, thinking
that now we will get this one who was going to address us.
As I was standing there, I saw the police armed with firearms,
lining up. I thought that they were paying respects to this big
man who was going to come. There was a European who was

not dressed in uniform. He called a young non-European from outside. He said "Come here, you! Come here, you!" This man tried to find his way through the people in order to go to this man who was calling him. When this man, this young man, got close to the gate, this European opened the gate, caught hold of this young man, jerked him about, pushed him inside. This young man's hat fell off. I saw this young man pointing at his hat, where it had fallen off.

The Chairman: What sort of hat was it? — An ordinary hat. The two of them came back. The European allowed him to pick up this hat.

What do you mean by an "ordinary" hat; the type that you see here? — Not a cap; a hat — similar to that hat, there.

That is an ordinary felt hat?— It was a grey hat. Then he escorted him. When he got into the gate, he was kicked, and pushed inside. A non-European young man was walking on the inside of the fence. He tried to get the people to stand back, not to lean up against the fence. After they had finished putting that man in, they then said to this man that was trying to get the people to stand back, not to lean against the fence. They said to him, "Go out!" As he was about to get out at the gate, they rushed at him. One of the policemen had some pips on his shoulder, and a little stick. He came out, pursued this man.

Examination continued:

Outside the gate? — Yes. Into the crowd. The crowd opened up. Now they were going towards the gate which leads to the clinic. He left him alone, and he came back. When this European came back, when he was in the centre of the tarmac road, he saw a little stone [indicates].

The Chairman: That is slightly larger than a cricket ball, I suppose? — About the size of a tennis ball; but it was not as round as a tennis ball. He picked it up, he threatened this man, as if to throw, but this young man ran away amongst the people towards the cafés. After this young man had run away towards the cafés, the Europeans inside spoke and said *Loop julle! Loop julle!* ["Get a move on!"] *Hamba* ["Go"] — in Zulu. The people then spread — they opened up and they spread. This white man that came outside, just as he got inside the gate, I heard the voice over there saying *"Skiet!"* ["Shoot!"] Then shots were fired.

Examination continued:

The man who came outside the gate, how was he dressed? — He had a pair of trousers on which has the same colour as the trousers worn by that constable, there [khaki]. And he had a cap similar to that worn by a policeman [peak cap]. He had a shirt on, not a jacket.

Did he have pips on his shoulders, too! — I think there were crowns. They are similar to a crown. They were nearly similar in colour as the clothing he had on.

And did this man have a stick? — Yes, a short little stick, as indicated.

Was this the same man as you previously described as having a stick? — Yes.

Then you heard someone shout *"Skiet!"* and then, what happened? — And you could hear the rifles, the report.

And what did you do, then, when you heard that? — I did not get frightened at all. I thought it was only blank cartridges that they were firing. At that time, I was facing towards the gate. When I was about a mile to go to the café, I saw a person; as I turned, I saw a male, non-European, lying on the ground, as far as from here to the desk just behind Mr. Claassen, there. [Six paces.] Just at that time, I felt a bullet grazing my trousers, like this. It did not go in — on my right leg. The trousers were torn. Then I got a fright. I thought to myself "Hah! Are they shooting in fact?" Just as I lifted my left leg to go forward, I was struck by a bullet here, in the right hip, and I dropped. Then they fired. Just at that stage, I heard something sounding like a mouth organ — not like a whistling sound, but like a mouth organ. It went "Pie-ie-ie-ie-ie-ieng." It kept quiet; then they were shooting at that time; and again, the same noise, and they kept quiet. When this noise was made the first time, this "Pie-ie-ie-ie-ieng," they fired. Pa-pa-pa! Then the second sound came; then they ceased firing.

Before this firing, did the crowd try to get into the Police Station? — I did not see the crowd trying to get in at the gate. Or anywhere else? — I don't know, towards the back, where the fence is, whether they tried to get in there. Not in front. I did not see them trying to get in there.

After the shooting started, what did most of the people still do? — They ran away.

After you were shot, you were lying on the ground? — I fell, and I lay on the ground.

After the shooting, did anyone come to speak to you? — They did not come near me. Just after they ceased firing, a European came along. He had something round, like this, but longer, and a small one, like this; it had a little rod attached to it, which fits into this big one. The big one he had in his hand. The small one he held in front of his mouth. He spoke through that. Also the policemen were going towards the gate. He spoke again, then they turned back. One of the police mounted the Saracen and sat on top of the Saracen.

Was that after the shooting had stopped? — Yes.

Could you see from where you were lying? — Yes; I could. When they ceased firing, a non-European by the name of Moto came from the café's side, from the people who were there

at the café's side. He had his hand raised like this [indicates]. One of the police, or both, that were sitting on the Saracens, said, *"Jy moet 'n wit sakdoek om daardie hand van jou sit; ons skiet jou nou dood, bliksem!"* ["You should put a white hand-kerchief round that hand of yours; we will shoot you dead now, scoundrel."] This man did not speak. He just passed this gentleman. When he got to the gate, my face was facing towards the café. I tried by turning my head to see where this man was going to. When he got in front of the gate, some of the Europeans asked him, *"Waar gaan jy?"* ["Where are you going?"] He then replied, *"Kyk, baas hoe 18 die mense dood; wat het hulle gemaak? Niks!"* ["Look, baas, eighteen people are dead; what did they do? Nothing!"] *"Loop," se hy. "Hoekom het jy nie eerder met jou eie mense gepraat nie! Loop!"* ["Go," says he. "Why did you not talk to your own people before! Go!"] That man then walked past at my feet. He went back to the group of non-Europeans. A European policeman who had said he must put a white rag round his hand, or a white handkerchief, pointed at me. He said, *"Hierdie hond — ons het hom niks gemaak nie; kyk, hy kou nog."* ["This dog, we've done nothing to him; look, he's still chewing."]
Where was he standing when he said that? — He was sitting on the bonnet of one of the Saracens. He said to me, *"Staan op, jong, loop! Ons het jou niks gemaak nie!"* ["Stand up, man, be off! We have done nothing to you!"] I then pointed to him here, where I was wounded. It was not bleeding at the time, but something was protruding. It looked like fat. He then said, "It is not bleeding from there; if you don't want to get up from here, we will kill you now." I remained silent, and I just looked at him. Another European was behind him and he said, *"Here! kyk hoe le hulle dood, kerels!"* ["God! Look how they lie dead, fellows!"]
After that man said what you have told us, what happened to

you? — This man then instructed the lorries to be brought out and I also heard him saying, *"Bel op die ambulans, kerels, dat hulle kom laai!"* ["Ring up the ambulance, fellows, for them to come and load."] Then a non-European policeman came to me. Some of them caught hold of me by the lower portion of my body and the others by the arms, to get me out of the way. Then they caught hold of me, on my right leg, and I felt pain. I said, "No, leave me alone, here." "[?] come here!" They sent her to me and I put my hands round her shoulders as indicated. They took me across the street and put me next to the clinic fence. After they put me down there, there was a lorry that had arrived there. That is one of the police lorries. They then took the corpses of those who were dead, put them into the lorry, loaded them into the lorry. This man—while they were loading this non-European man, Moto — there were many people walking about where these dead people were lying and I saw him also walking about there — Europeans and police, too. When this non-European crossed the street onto the eastern side, another European policeman said, in Afrikaans, *"Daardie man is altyd hier tussen die mense; ek dink hy is ook een van die moeilikheidmakers."* ["That man is always here among the people; I think he is also one of the trouble-makers."] There was a European, who was dressed in blue, but that was a uniform, and one of these soldiers' helmets or caps — the small one. He said to this policeman, *"Waffer eene?"* ["Which one?"] I heard him saying, *"Daardie een met die blou pak, Kolonel."* ["That one in the blue suit, Colonel."] This one who is called colonel then said, *"Roep daardie man! Roep daardie man!"* ["Call that man!"] He was then called, he came. As he was coming, it was said "put him inside." This European then caught hold of this young non-European, who was not dressed in uniform. He said to him, "Do you know me?" "Yes, sir, I know you very well." He said, "Now, why are you always here?" Moto said, "No, but I have just arrived. I am coming from work and I found it to be in a position it is in now. Just as I arrived, you finished firing." He was then locked up.

Were you then taken to hospital? — After that, an ambulance arrived and I was then removed to hospital.

And you have been in hospital ever since? — Yes.

What happened to your leg? — I don't know; but when I was told by this European to get up, I tried to and I found that my right leg was just hanging loose.

You are here in Baragwanath Hospital with your leg in fractions, and it is torn? — That is so.

I just want to ask you something again about the crowd before the shooting. What was the mood of this crowd; was it a wild crowd, for instance? — The way I saw them, to me they appeared to be pleased. They said, "We have trouble with regard to the passes, and we just want to hear; to hear what the Europeans have to say about it."

Did it strike you that this crowd was a very angry crowd and wanted to attack the police? — They were practically round the Police Station, but where I was, I did not see anything wrong being done, such as to indicate that the people were annoyed, where I was, or that they wanted to fight or anything like that. There was no one who had a stick. People that had little sticks were using that walking, to assist them when they were walking.

Are you able to tell the Commissioner — I don't know whether you are — did you have the impression that there were other people there, like yourself, because people had ordered them to go there? — I would say so.

No further questions.

Re-examination: No questions.

The Chairman: When did you first hear that there was going to be a demonstration or a gathering on Monday, the 21st? — I heard that on Friday.

Did people tell you, or did you get a pamphlet? — I heard at work.

That morning, that is now before eleven o'clock, that is before the aeroplanes flew over, did you either yourself become aware of the fact that there was unrest in the township, or did you hear from what others were saying that there had been trouble earlier that morning — I could see that myself, but I did not know it might be something serious.

Had you heard any shooting? — No; not at that time.

In your evidence you referred to the fact that some group had accused you of wanting to run away from the meeting when you wanted to go and relieve yourself? — Yes.

And then I think you told me that they said something to the effect that they did not want to cause trouble, but if you didn't listen you might be injured? — Yes.

I want to ask you, what did you understand by that? — Sunday afternoon, while I was busy working with the bus, there were some people standing at the bus stop. They had some little notes — on that little paper there was written "P.A.C."

That is in the buttonhole? — No; it was pinned, here, to the lapel. They said "We beg you, our people, tomorrow we must be just as one. We are not going to fight with the Europeans. We just want to ask them to alter this pass law because it is hard on us." They also said "Is a person running away from work, if he is going to work?" It was also said that if a person is woken up and he does not want to get up, he will be in trouble "because we will lay our hands on him." "Tomorrow we want all the men including the women, to be at the same place because the women are also carrying passes." That caused me not to be against it but to go along with them, is because it was said "If you run away, you might get hurt."

Injured by whom? — They only said "We will lay our hands on the one that does not want to."

Are those the people who spoke to you? — I am talking about the people who were talking at the bus stop. In other words, I think they were organising.

On this Sunday when you heard this at the bus stop, did you then understand where you had to be the next day? — Not at that time. I then thought to myself that they might go to the big Police Station in town.

Which town would that be? — Vereeniging.

Why did you think so? — I just had that thought because that is where the big authorities are.

Do you know whether anybody else also thought that was where you would make your protest? — No.

These people who spoke to you on the Sunday, did they give you any idea what would happen on Monday? — They weren't speaking to me. They were speaking in general, to all the people that were there; not to me personally.

No, I know; I understand that. But you were told that you must all be as one? — I said so.

Did you also understand from what was being said, how you were to act as one or be as one? — It was said that they wanted the men and women as well not to go to work; they want them all to be present, and certain persons will be elected to speak about the passes.

But did you know on that Sunday, from what was being said there, where you had to collect? — No; I did not.

Was there no mention in this talk that was going on on the

Sunday, that you would meet at the football ground or you would meet at the Police Station or you would meet at the Superintendent's office? — No. It was said that we would go to the Police Station, but it was not mentioned which Police Station that we were going to go to, at eight o'clock in the morning; we would go steadily to the Police Station, but it was not mentioned which Police Station we had to go to.

You say the idea was that you had to be at the Police Station at eight o'clock? — No. They said that we must walk steadily up to the Police Station at eight o'clock; not to be at the Police Station at eight.

You had to get together at about that time and then walk steadily to the Police Station? — Yes.

When did you first find out that the Police Station at which you had to meet was the Sharpeville Police Station? — The next morning, when I came to the trees — when I came from the trees.

When was that? — It was close to nine o'clock in the morning. When you came back from the trees at nine o'clock or thereabouts, did you hear what had been happening earlier that morning in Seeiso Street? — Yes; I heard that it was said that the Police were assaulting the people where the Location starts, where the buildings are erected with these certain kind of bricks, which is called the "mompara" brick.

Did you hear anything more about what had happened there? — The people who spoke mostly were women. For instance, one would hear a woman say to another, "Oh, my husband has been assaulted by the police." I saw another man who had a shop there at the hostel; he had an injury here [indicates]. He also said that he had been injured by the police.

Where was this; did he tell you where he had been injured? — There, at the shop.

Now, I have had some evidence here, and I have seen it myself, that the fence on the western side and on the southern side of the Police Station had been pushed over to some extent? — I cannot deny that this could have happened because people at the back were anxious to see what was happening in front, and they might have pushed forward.

Did you see any tendency for them to do that, or is that merely an opinion that you express? — I saw that they were moving forward, trying to see what was happening in front, because on the righthand side of the gate, facing towards the clinic — some time, as we were all standing there, one of the Saracens amongst the other Saracens — this Saracen went round collecting cars and lorries, and bringing them to the Police Station. This Saracen was ahead of these vehicles as they were proceeding to the Police Station. People were standing there when this vehicle came to the Police Station. They were standing in the street as well. They then blocked up the road. These vehicles had to come to where the gate is, with the Saracen. The gate would have been about as far as from here to the end of the screen, behind the gentleman with the green jersey on [plus or minus fifteen paces]. The Saracen came along as if it was going towards these people that were standing at the fence. The people who were standing in the road, opened up the road. It came down, out of the road as if it was going on to them. Then they ran towards the other people that were standing there, pressing up against the fence, because they were running away from this Saracen, the one that went out of the road, as it was coming forward. I think the Saracen did that three times. If it comes there with one of the vehicles, if the vehicle goes into the yard it goes down to where the station — where the Location starts; I do not know whether there is an office, or not — to the office; I don't know whether it goes to the office or not. It comes there with vehicles and goes back again, comes back again with vehicles and so on.

I also had evidence that at a very late stage, that is very shortly before the shooting, it appeared as if people at the gate came into the police yard some short distance? — I have said there was a little time that I had gone to the café. I don't know whether that happened during my absence to the café. But when I returned from the café, I did not see such a thing happen.

Apart from whether anybody wanted to get into the police grounds, was there any tendency opposite the gate, perhaps, for people from behind to push so hard that the people at the gate could not help themselves, that they were pushed into the police grounds, when the gate was opened? I don't want your opinion. If you did not see anything like that, you can just tell me. — As I say, I don't know whether that happened during my absence to the café; but when I came back from the café, people moved backwards.

Did you sense that there was some annoyance on the part of the people in that part of the crowd because of the way in which the police were behaving? — No. I don't know all the people. I know some of them by sight.

No, I mean just the people around you; you could not know all of them? — I am also referring to those people. If a person speaks, I heard someone saying to those who were standing there, "Don't be frightened of the Europeans; just be calm. We want to hear. We don't want any noise." I mean, "Don't swear at them."

Did you hear some people swearing? — No. I cannot say yes, that I did hear one swearing at the police. This Sesutu language, I don't know that very well.

After the shooting had finished, did you see the police? You said already you saw the police moving about the crowd. Did you see anybody giving assistance to the people who were lying there, the wounded? — The crowd as such wanted to run to the assistance of the wounded who were lying there, but they were chased away by the police. The people that I saw assisting the people, also the dead, were ministers.

Were there no police assisting any of the injured? — That is the work that was done by the police, namely assisting.

*   *   *

ELIAS LELIA, *sworn, states (through Interpreter)*:
                    (Indemnity explained to Witness.)
                    (Evidence now given without Interpreter.)

Examination by Mr. Plewman:

You are not a member of any political organisation, are you? — No.

And your standard of education is junior certificate? — Yes.

And you run your own business as a dress designer? — Yes.

You live in Sharpeville? — Yes.

With your mother and your sister? — Yes.

We are concerned with the events of the 21st, which is the Monday. Have you any knowledge of the happenings in Sharpeville on the Sunday night? — I have.

Can you tell me what you know and then how you came to this knowledge, and why you were interested? — I read about it and I heard about it, from rumours, that there would be something in Sharpeville, like an anti-pass campaign.

As a result of that, just tell me when you went out on the Sunday night and what you then saw? — I went out at eight P.M. on Sunday to Qwadi's meeting; a person by the name of Qwadi was addressing that meeting. I knew him to be a member of the P.A.C. but I did not know his official position.

What were the activities that night, after the meeting? — After the meeting, there was nothing except that the meeting, while it was still going on the police came and scattered it.

As a result of that dispersal, what did you do? — I went straight back home.

The Chairman: Just tell me, where did that meeting take place? — In Sharpeville.

At what particular place? — I can't say, really. It was on the outskirts of Sharpeville.

Near to the Municipal offices? — Near to Site and Service on the eastern side of it.

Examination continued:

Just in fairness to you, will you say what your interest was in all these activities? — Certainly. I do write in my spare time.

And were you collecting information as to what was happening for the purpose of your writing? — Of my writing.

And were you making notes? — I was.

Those notes we have not been able to find. You say you then went back to bed; and did you sleep the rest of the night, at home? — Yes.

What time did you get up the next morning? — I woke up a little earlier than six-thirty, because I left home at six-thirty to have a shower in the change-house.

You have communal shower houses at Sharpeville and you went to one of those communal shower houses? — Yes.

In doing so, did you see anything of the position in Seeiso Street, the main street of Sharpeville? — I live far from Seeiso Street. I am in Zwane Street.

Well, perhaps you will then just tell his Worship what you noticed on getting up at six-thirty and going to this communal shower? — On the road, I saw nothing, until I had had the shower. In the shower room I heard rumours that people had been molested who had tried to go to work, on Monday.

As a result of that? — I had to take my bike and I went to Seeiso Street.

You heard the rumours when having your shower, and then you took a bicycle and went to see what was happening in Seeiso Street? — That's right.

And what did you find in Seeiso Street? — I went to the bus terminus and there I found nothing of the sort. I only found that the people were more than usual, but not too much.

You found there were more people than usual standing about? — Going about. From there, I stood there maybe half an hour, before I went back home again.

And anything that you noticed that you think we should know about? — From there I went back again down Seeiso Street, and when I was near the school square, when I threw my eyes down Seeiso Street I saw a group of about five hundred.

What did you then do there; did you find anyone else you knew? — From that point, I turned back towards home, not exactly home, but to the Police Station.

What took you to the Police Station? — More people were moving towards the Police Station.

Did anything happen in Seeiso Street while you were there that you can tell us about, or did you just go straight back to the Police Station? — Nothing happened.

At the Police Station, did you find anyone you knew? — Yes.

The Chairman: About what time did you get to the Police Station? — It was just before eight.

Examination continued:

Was there a crowd at the Police Station when you got there? — Yes.

About how many people, do you think? — Well, I did not attend much to the crowd.

What happened at the Police Station? — I took my bike home and came back to the Police Station, just to find that the group of people were increasing rapidly.

What did you then do? — I started taking my notes.

Did you find anyone you knew at the Police Station? — Yes; this was Qwadi.

Did Qwadi say anything to you there? — Not at that moment.

At any other time, later on? — He came to me because he knew me very well and told me that he heard the rumour saying that the people were blocking the road.

Which road was that? — Seeiso Street.

As a result of that, what did you do? — As a result of that, I followed him.

And where did you go? — Down Seeiso Street, to the crowd.

Where did you find the crowd — at what point in Seeiso Street? — At the school square.

The same school square that you referred to before? — Yes.

And can you estimate the size of the crowd at all? — The size of the crowd was about seven hundred, and the crowd that came with us down to Seeiso Street from the Police Station.

What was the purpose of your going to Seeiso Street? — To go and witness.

To see what was happening? — Yes.

Do you know whether there were any complaints about what was happening, or what the attitude of the people was or what Qwadi's purpose was in going there? — When we came there, the people told us that the police were not willing to go to the Police Station; but they were waiting for them to march together to the Police Station.

Was that a statement made to you by the people in Seeiso

Street? — That is right. Then, ten minutes later Qwadi came
to me and told me that the police said they were not prepared
to make any move at the people who were blocking the road.
Then he told me that he was going to tell the people to move
up to the Police Station.

So, as far as you knew, were the people then persuaded to move
in the direction of the Police Station, and did they in fact do
so? — They did.

Did you go back to the Police Station directly? — I took the
bike home first.

And then you went back to the Police Station? — Back to the
Police Station.

The Chairman: About what time was this that you got to Seeiso
Street and had these discussions about the crowd moving off
to Sharpeville Police Station? — It was about, if not exactly
ten o'clock.

Examination continued:

So when you got back to the Police Station, that was a little
after ten? — Yes.

Whereabouts did you stand or go at the Police Station? — My
first trouble was that I did not have standing place. I went up
and down, moved through the people, until the first arrival of
the police.

Until the first police vehicles? — No; they came in a group —
minus those who came singly.

Are you inferring that these were the people coming from the
crowd in Seeiso Street? — No; the police. They came round
Zwane Street.

Did they take up position anywhere? — Immediately where the
Police Station premises end.

In Zwane Street? — In Zwane Street.

That is on the southeastern side of the Police Station? — In Zwane Street, yes.

Did any other police arrive while you were there? — Yes.

Who else came? — Saracens, and then the planes; but I can't really say whether the planes came before the Saracens, or whether the Saracens came before the planes.

Whereabouts were you when the aeroplanes came over? — I was still in Zwane Street, walking up and down between the people and the police, trying to see that they would not provoke the police.

Why were you doing that? — I did it, I can say, in moral support of the P.A.C.

You did it sort of to assist the P.A.C. there? — Yes.

Had you been asked to do that or did you think it necessary or why did you do that? — At that point, we were not asked.

And did you just think it incumbent on you to do something to keep order? — That's right. I wanted to know what would be the outcome of the P.A.C.'s campaign and it was my duty.

Did you you notice any of the P.A.C. leaders speaking to the police inside the police grounds? — That was Tsolo.

And who was he speaking to at the time when you looked? — He was speaking to a man, first in a grey suit and with a hat on. I don't know his name.

Whereabouts was this discussion taking place? — They were in the southern part of the Police Station — in the entrance of the Police Station.

Opposite the little gate? — Yes.

And were you anywhere near there? — I was near the little gate at the time that the discussion took place.

After the discussion, did anything happen; did Tsolo come to you or say anything? — He came to me and told me that the police — that is to say the man he was talking to — was complaining about the crowd leaning against the fence. He told me that I should try to keep the people off the fence.

Did he say anything else to you about people who should stay there or what the plan was that the police had? — Not at that moment.

At any other time? — He came and told me, "You shall have your answer at two o'clock," as there was a man from Pretoria who would come and address the people.

Was that a statement made to you particularly, or to the crowd in general? — Well, I was talking to him in particular.

So it was something he said to you? — That's right.

Did you try to keep the people off the fence? — I did.

How did you do that? — By pressing between the people and the fence, walking up and down.

I wonder if you will have a look at Exhibit "B1" and perhaps indicate in what area you did that? Exhibit "B1" is an aerial photograph of the Police Station taken some time during the course of that morning. — Only between the two gates [witness indicates].

You moved between the crowd and the fence along the fence, between the two gates; that is from the southern fence from the small gate, and up as far as the large gate on the western side? — Yes.

Did you have any difficulty in keeping that crowd off the fence; did you have any difficulty in moving between them and the fence? — At first, but as I kept on — *ek het tussen hulle en die draad so effentijies deurgedruk. Nie te veel nie.* ["I pushed a little between them and the fence. Not too much."]

Can you tell me, when the aeroplanes dived low over that part of the township, did that have any effect, that you noticed? — Many people ran away, but as they were running away more people came out from various places.

So you think the other people were attracted? — Yes.

Was there any hostility in the crowd at that stage? — Not that I saw.

Was anyone else trying to keep the crowd in order? — I could not see; I was also busy myself.

Do you know whether there were any people inside the police grounds at that stage? I am talking about Africans. — I only saw Qwadi.

During the time that you were there, did police vehicles arrive at different times? — Yes.

And they went in, we understand, at the western gate? — Yes.

And took up various positions inside the police grounds? — Yes.

I think we have it in evidence that the Saracens were at some stage drawn up at various points, some facing north, the northwestern corner, and some — one facing South? — Yes.

You noticed all that? — That I noticed.

Did you see any arrests taking place? — I only saw one, and that was Tsolo's.

What position were you in at that time, in relation to the fence; more or less where were you? — I should say I was near the southeastern corner.

Was there any reaction from the crowd when that arrest took place? — No.

Not that you know of? — Not that I know of.

Was that before, or after the police had been drawn up into a line facing the western fence? — I can't distinguish that.

You are not sure? — Not sure.

Do you remember that the police were at some stage drawn up in a line? — Yes.

If we now come to the shooting, do you remember how the shooting started; did you see how it started? — Well, I should say I heard the shots, as I was looking at the police.

Do you know what gave rise to the shooting; did you see any incident that you could tell his Lordship about, that gave rise to it? — No.

And you heard the shots. Now, I would like you to give me some particulars about the shooting you heard, did that come from the police on the western side? — Yes.

And how did the shooting sound to you — continuous, isolated shots? — Well, they were in a volley, with two gaps between them.

That is a volley, a gap, another volley, a gap and another volley? — The last volley was not exactly a volley; it was shots, as if they were aiming.

When the shooting started, what did you do? — The first shooting when it occurred, I remained stunned at my place. I was then opposite the building corner.

Is that the corner nearest to the . . . ? — To the small gate.

. . . to the western side, or between the small gate and the corner? — Yes.

The Chairman: Could you perhaps again on that photograph show us where you stood when the shooting started — right at the corner? — Yes; not at . . .

Examination continued:

You indicate a place on the southern fence, opposite the corner of the building line of the Police Station? — Yes.

You were standing there when the shooting started, and now tell us exactly what you did? — As I have already said, I remained stunned when the first shooting took place. When the second volley came, I ran away, eastwards.

Along the fence? — Yes.

And from that point, which way did you run? — I went around the Police Station.

That is the fence on the south side? — Yes. Then I was about at the eastern corner, when the shooting stopped.

That is round the fence on the eastern side? — On the eastern side, yes.

And you were about where when the shooting started? — About the eastern corner.

Perhaps you can show me on the photograph? — [Witness indicates.]

You were about on the northeastern corner of the Police Station? — Yes.

Is that where you were when the shooting stopped? — Yes.

Now, I wonder if you can — one knows the difficulties, but can you give an estimate of how long the shooting lasted altogether; the first shot, to the last shot? — If I am not wrong, I should say it was about a minute.

The Chairman: Did you [inaudible] from where you were? — No, I was running.

You say you were stunned when the shooting started? — That's right.

It is not an easy matter, but have you got any idea how soon after the shooting started you started running down Zwane Street? — Immediately; on the second volley.

Would that be a matter of a few seconds after the shooting started, or longer? How long did you remain standing? — After the first shooting?

Yes; when you heard the shots, then you say you remained, you were stunned? — That's right.

And then I understand you to say you ran eastwards along Zwane Street? — When the second volley took place.

How long was the first burst? — That I can't estimate.

Could you estimate it this way: Was it a very short burst, or was it a long burst? — It was a very short burst.

Then you started running? — Yes.

Did you continue running until you reached the spot that you indicated? — When I ran, it was when the first volley took place. Then I could hear that they were still shooting.

You ran round to the northeast corner of the Police Station and when you reached that point you say the shooting stopped? — Yes.

What I want to know is, from the time that you started running until you got there, did you keep on running or did you stop right away? — I kept on running.

Examination continued:

What happened to the crowd on the southern side where you were standing, when the shooting started? — They were also running away.

In which direction were they running? — In all directions.

Some in the same direction as you? — Yes.

After the shooting had stopped, you told us what your position was. Did you move up that northern fence in the direction of the clinic? — Yes.

And in that field to the north of the Police Station, did you notice anything? — I noticed many people I knew. The first one was lying on the northwestern corner of the Police Station. That was Malefaan. And a few paces in front of him, that is to say in the tarred road, there lay another man I also knew who stays opposite me, and that was Milane. The second one was lying in the tarred road running along the western fence of the Police Station.

I take it you saw a lot of other bodies as well? — Yes.

Can you just say where you think most of them were? — As I

could see, most of them were in front of the Police Station—
between the Police Station and the clinic, and in the field as
well; the open space between the cafés and . . .

The Chairman: That is to the northwest of the Police Station?
— Yes.

Examination continued:

Did you go into that field at all? — I did. There lay about
thirty people.

Were they all dead, or were they dead and wounded? —
Others were dead, others were on the dying side, others were
just wounded.

Did you find anyone else you knew there? — From the field,
when I came back, I saw somebody I knew who was lying on
the eastern corner of the clinic.

Was that somebody by the name of Massila? — Yes.

You tried to help him? — He was already gone.

You mean he was dead? — He was dead.

Did you do anything to assist any of the other people there? —
That I did, but the police stopped us.

What did the police say to you? — They just told me to go
away, it was not my business.

In which direction did you go? — I did not take that word too
much; I kept on moving about the people.

You mean you continued notwithstanding? — Yes.

And when you say you went about the people, did you move
in any particular direction? — I went near the fence.

Which fence is that? — The police fence.

And in which direction did you go; towards Zwane Street,
or . . . ? — Towards Zwane Street, and on the sidewalk I
found another boy I knew by the name of Stephen Lohobo with

a bullet wound in his thigh. The bullet looked so small that I thought it was a revolver, because a revolver is a very small weapon.

You think a revolver is a smaller weapon than another firearm? — Yes.

This man has been a witness here. Was there anything else that took place about that time? — From that position, I went again over the street, across the street . . .

Which street is that? — In front of the Police Station; on its corner, which is Zwane Street, there I found another two girls, one shot and one complaining that the people trampled over her. From there, I went into Zwane Street, eastwards, where I found a man lying on the island.

Yes? — By the name of Mapeke, almost dying.

While you were there, was there anybody else lying where he was lying? — A policeman came there and he said to him, *"Ja, nou gaan jy na Mayeboye-toe."* ["Yes, now you are going to Mayeboye." *]

Was that a European policeman or a non-European policeman? — A European police.

Did you hear any other statements from the police while you were there, or at any earlier stage? — In the earlier stages while I was still moving amongst the bodies which were lying in the street, I heard a man — a non-European by the name of Ben Pitso, shouting and saying, *"Ja, ek het julle gese die Polisie sal skiet. Daar het julle dit; vat dit; dit is julle Afrika daardie."* ["Yes, I told you the police would shoot. There you have it; take it; that is your Africa."]

Did you ever hear him saying anything like that before? — No.

Can you also tell me, as you moved through the people there

* This is a reference to an A.N.C. Slogan: Africa belongs to me.

did you notice any weapons lying about in the street?
— No.

Was there anything lying about in the street? — Shoes, hats
and a few umbrellas.

You did not see anything that you would call a weapon?
— No.

Did you stand around there until the ambulances came?
— Yes.

Did you notice anything in particular about the ambulances?
— Yes.

What was that? — Others were from Johannesburg.

You noticed some of them had the Johannesburg registration
number on? — Yes.

And how long do you think it took until everybody had been
picked up there or helped? — Say about forty minutes.

The Chairman: In your estimation, when did the first ambulance arrive? — I would say about ten minutes after the
shooting.

And you say from then it was forty minutes before the last of
the injured had been removed? — All the ambulances which
took part in the picking up of the bodies, let's say the wounded;
they all came at one time.

Oh, did the ambulances all arrive together? — Yes.

And you say they were there within ten minutes? — Yes. In
my estimation.

I know it is an estimate. But you say from then on until the
time that the last ambulance moved off with the last of the
injured that was forty minutes? — Yes. They started first with
the dead.

The ambulances? — No; the police vans, while the ambulances
were still waiting.

In that space of ten minutes? — No. The ambulances came

between the ten minutes space, and then, while they were still on the way, I should say, the bodies were being picked up. Only those that were dead and a few of the injured which were helped in the private cars and taxis.

I see; there were some private cars and taxis before the ambulances came? — Yes.

Were some of the injured removed with the cars? — Yes.

Then you say dead were being loaded . . . ? — Loaded into police vans.

Examination continued:

Now, I want to go back again to your experience with the crowds throughout the period that you were near to the Police Station. Was there anything at any stage that made you think that the crowd wanted to attack the police? — No. The crowd was very much under control.

Was it a hostile, aggressive crowd? — Very humble.

Was there any singing and shouting going on? — Well, singing was here and there, and the shouting of "Afrika!" was very occasional.

So far as you are concerned, can you give any reason why the shooting should have taken place? Did you see anything or hear anything that could have led to the shooting? — In my own opinion?

Yes. — Yes I think I can. What I say might not be suitable to your ears, but I think I must say it, if I would be allowed. *The Chairman:* I have told you, you are free to say anything you want to say. — Well, as far as I could judge the shooting was prejudiced on a political basis, supported by hatred, *baas-skap* and discrimination.

Examination continued:

Is that your view of perhaps underlying causes? — Yes.

Apart from underlying causes, did you see any incident or any-thing like that? — Nothing of the sort.

And as you moved through the crowd, also between the fence and the Police Station, did you notice whether there were peo-ple armed, anxious to get at the police? — Not at any moment.

*   *   *

BENEDICT GRIFFITHS, *sworn, states (through Interpreter):*

Examined by Mr. Plewman:

Benedict, you live in Sharpeville? — Yes, I do.

You live with your parents? — Yes, I do.

What is your father's occupation? — He is a member of the S.A. Police.

Do you work yourself? — The day I got injured was the day I had started work.

You got injured at the Police Station at Sharpeville? — Yes.

Do you remember the aeroplanes flying low over the Police Station? — I do.

Were you then at the Police Station? — I was there at the time.

Did you go to the Police Station? I know there was a crowd there, but did you go by yourself, or did you go with friends? — There were many of us that went there.

But to that place, did you go alone? — Yes; I was alone.

And what did you go there for? — Because we were prevented from going to work. I was going to listen to what was going to be said at the Police Station.

I want you to try and tell me where you stood at the Police Station, if you can. Were you standing on the café side or were you standing on the side of the big street, Zwane Street? — I was standing on the big street side.

Which street is that; is that the street between the Police Station and the clinic, or another street? — The one between the clinic and the Police Station.

And do you know that there is a gate in that fence of the Police Station where the vehicles go through? — Yes; I do.

How near did you get to that gate? — I was about as far from it as from here to that lady sitting there. [Six to seven paces.]

And how near to the wire itself were you? — I was just on the side of the fence; I was not leaning up against the fence.

How many people were there between where you were and the fence? How many people were in front of you? — Not many; about two.

Did you see many vehicles arrive there? — Yes, I did.

Some of them were lorries, some of them were Saracens, some of them were ordinary cars? — Yes.

And did you see policemen getting out of these vehicles? — Yes. At a later stage, did you see the policemen inside the police fence standing up and forming a line? — Yes; inside the Police Station fence.

And they were facing the people standing outside the fence? — Yes. They were facing the people standing outside the fence.

Did you see them, whether they had weapons? — Yes; I did.

What did they have, guns? — They had guns and other weapons that I had seen for the first time; they were sort of like iron weapons.

And did you see them loading these guns at any stage? — Yes; I did.

When they loaded the guns, did you think there was any danger, or did you fear them in any way? — When I saw them loading the guns, then I started getting frightened.

Did you think they were going to shoot you? — No; I did not

think that they were going to shoot me, but I thought they were just frightening us.

Did you go away from that place, or did you stay there? — I got a fright when I saw there was a person inside the fence, trying to prevent the people from standing up against the fence.

Did you see anything happen to that person? — I saw them putting him into the Police Station.

Was that the only person you saw them taking into the Police Station? — No; another one was caught hold of afterwards.

The second one, how did they catch hold of him? — They were jerking him about.

What did the crowd do at that stage? — When the people saw that this man was being jerked about, they tried to run away, and it could be seen, then, that there was no one who was going to address the gathering, but they were wanting to fight with the gathering.

Did anything else happen at about that time? — Yes.

What happened? — A sergeant who spoke to the police that were standing in the line said to them *"Skiet!"* ["Shoot!"]

When that happened, did the police then shoot? — Yes; they fired.

What did the people round you do? — We all ran away.

Did you also run? — Yes; I did.

In which direction did you run? — I ran in the direction of a place called Zinzele.

Is that towards that big street, with the island? — That is correct.

South? — Yes.

When did you receive your injuries? — Just as I was across the street, I fell down.

You continued lying there? — Where I had fallen, I lay.

While you were lying there, do you know if the shooting was

still going on? — They were still firing. The bullets were passing me, missing me where I was lying.

Did they eventually stop shooting altogether? — Yes; they did. Then, did you look up and see that there were many people lying in the street? — Yes.

I want to come back to the time just before the shooting started. Was it your impression, then, that the crowd was trying to attack the police? — No.

What was the crowd like immediately before the shooting? Perhaps I will just leave it to you to tell me what you thought the crowd was like? — They were happy and they were singing.

Did you see anybody near where you were, throwing stones at the police? — No. I did not see one.

After the shooting was all over and you were lying there, the police came out and they started taking the people nearer to the Police Station than you were, and eventually they also took you away and you were taken to hospital? — They first took the dead and put them to one side. We were taken by ambulance.

You have been in hospital ever since then? — Yes.

Just tell me what your age is? — Seventeen.

No further questions.

Re-examination: No questions.

The Chairman: Did I hear you correctly, namely that you are the son of a policeman? — Yes.

Is he a member of the South African Police? — Yes.

Where was he stationed at the time? — In Vereeniging.

He was not stationed at Sharpeville? — He was not stationed at Sharpeville; he was stationed at Vereeniging.

You are seventeen, but have you been to school? — I have been to school.

What standard did you pass? — Four.

And what employment were you going to take up on the Monday? — I was given a piece of paper as a substitute in case anyone does not come up to work, that I could be taken as a substitute.

Did you know that there was unrest during that night; that groups were going around to some houses, at least, and calling people to come out? — No.

You weren't disturbed? — No.

I am not quite certain; when did you go to the Police Station at Sharpeville? — Somewhere about one o'clock.

Where had you been that morning, up to one o'clock? — I was on my way to work that morning, and I was made to turn back.

Where were you made to turn back? — I had passed the brick and tile works, and I was near the big dam, there.

I am not quite sure where that is, so you will have to help me. Had you already got out of the Location? — Yes.

Where? — Lower down there are some new houses that have been erected there. I got as far as that, intending to go to work.

You did not go down Seeiso Street? — No.

Who made you turn back? — Oh, many people.

What did they say to make you turn back? — It was said that on that day no one is going to work, and if we refuse to turn back, not going to work — if we want to go to work, they will burn our passes. Then I turned back.

And then, did you go home? — Yes; I did.

And then, did you stay at home until you went to the Police Station? — Yes.

As you were standing in the crowd, there, did you hear anybody give expression to annoyance with the police? — No.

Not at all? — *Niks! Niks!*

Mr. Kentridge (through the Chairman): Benedict, did you see your father that morning? — Yes.

Where? — At home.

Was he off duty? — It was just the time that he had to go to work.

And did he go on duty? — Yes; but he was prevented.

DOCUMENTARY III

CHIEF LUTHULI'S CALL FOR A DAY
OF MOURNING

CHIEF LUTHULI

Calls upon you to:

- **MOURN THE VICTIMS OF POLICE VIOLENCE.**

- **PROTEST AGAINST POLICE KILLINGS.**

- **PROTEST AT THE PASS LAWS.**

STAY AT HOME
FOR ONE DAY
MONDAY 28th MARCH 1960

Issued by:- Chief A. J. Luthuli — Groutville — Natal.

GOLDPRINT